Car

"The force that through th
Drives my green age; that blasts the roots of trees
Is my destroyer. And I am dumb to tell the crooked rose
My youth is bent by the same wintry fever." -Dylan Thomas

The air of Oceanside, California was redolent with sagebrush and old dust. The earth there was dried, and when the rains came everything would sprout to life, and green fingers would push through cracks, contrasting sharply with the pale, dusty soil. This land was a metaphor for the personalities of my team members and for my own personality. It was as if we were all, like the cracked land, confined to a dusty limbo. It was as if now, since we had arrived in California, we were ready to grow. We packed our impossibly swollen duffels, shifted heavy cases of our sponsor's water—proudly labeled OWater—from the inside of the RV to the compartments underneath. By this point personalities had begun to show themselves a bit more clearly. I guessed, correctly it would turn out, that this entire race would be part adventure, part sociological experiment. It turned out at the end to be something of hybridization between a PBS documentary and a reality television program. Whether we were polishing and cleaning the bikes with old socks and toothbrushes or trying to appreciate the California sun, Hesselbarth, the photographer, took snapshots

1

of Chris Lake, Jim LaBelle, Chaney Becker, and Tim Bryant, the cyclists, lounging in the hot tubs, of team members frolicking in the waves of the Pacific, of all of us sitting in Rosia's, the Italian restaurant we frequented the few days we were in California before the race. Larger than life personalities began to creep to the surface.

News that Tim and Jim had been fighting over financial arrangements began to trickle down through the members of the team, distracting us from our goals.

Luckily, at that moment, we didn't realize how deeply some of the animosity had gone. It was a general truth then that none of us knew what was to come, which was probably for the best, for if we had known, many of us would've left that minute.

Pre-Ramble

What you and your lunatic friends will need if you are suddenly seized with the undeniable desire to abandon your families for fourteen days and follow an obsessive dream to compete in the trans-continental Race Across America in the unlikely quest to win the toughest bike race in the world:

1. Ten People Willing to Risk It All
2. Four Cyclists Who Have Each Trained for At Least a Year
3. Expensive Plane Tickets to California for All
4. Bikes that Weigh Almost Nothing but Cost a Fortune
5. One Recreational Vehicle, Rented with Insurance and Ready to Destroy
6. Two Minivans, Rented and Ready to Be Crashed
7. Craploads of Insurance
8. Tons of Bag Balm for the Cyclists', uh… "bags"
9. Cases and Cases of Expensive Bottled Water
10. A Bare Minimum of Ten Cups of Coffee, Per-Person, Per-Day
11. The Ability to Survive on Only Two Hours of Sleep Per-Day for Seven Days Straight
12. Tons and Tons of Cash to Piss Away on Fast

Food and Expensive Organic Stuff

13. Two Enormous Water Coolers Which You May Never Actually Use, and Which, Incidentally, You May Briefly Consider Using to Hold Human Waste

14. Two Additional Coolers for Food

15. Four Giant Speakers (two to mount on each minivan) That Can Be Duct-Taped to the Roof to Provide Tunes in the Middle of the Night for Weary Riders as They Glide Through the Middle of Many Nowheres, and for Sonically Assaulting Everything and Everyone

16. Bike Stands and Tools

17. Lots of Spare Parts

18. A Video Camera

19. Decent Life Insurance Policies

20. A Last Will and Testament

Per-Person Essentials: Crew

1. Sleeping Bag (You will lose this, so don't get attached.)
2. Pillow (To be thrown away the second you get back home.)
3. Headlamp with Extra Batteries (I highly recommend anything from Petzl, especially something with a colored lens for night time.)
4. Notebook
5. Pens/ Pencils/ Highlighters
6. Sunglasses (These will also get lost.)
7. Sun Block
8. Baseball Cap
9. Knit Hat (Things get cold at high altitudes, even in summer.)
10. Shorts
11. Pants
12. Short Sleeve Shirt (This too you will have to toss upon your return, for it will reek.)
13. Long Sleeve Shirt
14. Light Jacket/ Fleece
15. Rain Jacket
16. Socks
17. Underwear (Again, toss when you get

home.)

18.   Belt

19.   Bivy Sack or Small, One-Person Tent

20.   Water Bottles

21.   Cash

22.   Camera/ Batteries

23.   Toothbrush/ Paste

24.   Wet Wipes

25.   Powder

26.   Rain Jacket

27.   Anti-Fungal Powder

28.   Painkillers (Over the Counter—anything
      else, sadly, isn't allowed.)

29   Small First Aid Kit

30.   Sunglasses

31.   Eyeglasses (I wore contacts, but they were a
      pain and hurt my eyes.)

32.   Cell Phone

Per-Person Essentials (Cyclists)

(In addition to the aforementioned items for each crew member)

1. Extravagantly Expensive Bicycles, Ideally Two Each
2. Two Helmets
3. Specialized Cycling Clothing for Desert Heat, Freezing Rain, and Bitter Cold
4. Two Pairs of Expensive Clipless Cycling Shoes
5. Replacement Cleats for Shoes
6. Ten Water Bottles and Enough Water (We used Insulated Water Bottles, some with Gel Compartments Built In)
7. More Energy Gel, Energy Bars, and Powdered Energy Drink Mix than you can shake a stick at and more than you probably will ever wish to see again in your entire life.
8. Cycling Socks, loads of them
9. Mountains of Gold Bond Medicated Powder
10. Oodles of Bag Balm for the "Bags"
11. Duct Tape
12. Spare Sets of Wheels, Tires, and Tubes
13. Air Pumps

14.   CO2 Cartridges for Handheld Pumps

15.   Sunglasses

16.   Blackberry (a.k.a. Crackberry) Phone

17.   Flip Flops, to put on after long rides

18.   Customized Bike Jerseys that Cost a Fortune

19.   Fluffy and Comfortable Lounge Clothes

One

Remembering what happened during the Race Across America is—to say the very least—a bit tough. I'm reminded of what I've heard people say about living through the 1960s or going to Woodstock—If you can remember it, you weren't there. The same thing could easily be said of the RAAM. I've jogged memories out of my head by looking at photos, nudged them out by listening to recordings from interviews I'd made after it was over, and confronted them by watching video footage of our team. I've also talked to people who've endured what has been one of the most grueling and most rewarding experiences of our lives. Most people's memories are a bit hazy, indistinct, and muddled. But those from the RAAM, for most of us, have been reduced to near abstraction. If I said otherwise, I'd be lying.

Still, there are individual moments that stick out in their intensity, moments when I was—for one reason or another—particularly lucid, when I had one of the rarest things in an event such as this—ownership over the clarity of my mind. These moments were few, so the account in these pages is an approximation of reality, as is the case, I suppose, with almost any non-fiction account. But let me make it clear that this account is—by my own admission—flawed. Still, I have tried to capture what I can remember, to put down in writing the general feel and flavor of the race. I know that what I've written is true, even if the edges are blurred. I know that by the end our team was haggard, smeared into quick animal movements and headed towards a bright light in the distance of the future. I know that we were swaggering, full of the joy that runs through the veins of any such pure, intense, and ethereal existence.

The pages that follow are mostly my returns to the land of memory, where I have made an attempt—not to extract details—but to deduce truth, to filter through the detritus of the mind, and to reduce the whole experience to some whole that I, and perhaps others, can swallow—which has proved to be quite a feat indeed.

Two

The Race Across America prints posters every year promoting the race's arduous intensity, colossal magnitude, and what some would call its general and heartfelt insanity. I can attest that it is all of these things, and perhaps a bit more.

The RAAM, as it is known in cycling circles, has a cult following, particularly among those who relish the idea of pushing to the very brink of both physical and mental human endeavors. The race is, according to slogans on the posters, the "Toughest Bicycle Race in the World." By any standard this slogan is true, and it is also the reason so many bike-cult lunatics are drawn to the race. The 2009 RAAM poster made an additional claim: "This Ain't No Tour." The comment that race promoters were attempting to make to bike racers and enthusiasts, if not the rest of the world, was clear. The RAAM—unlike its very distant and better known cousin the Tour de France—is not a "stage race." It is a race of "truth." Stage races, like the Tour de France, may cover a great deal of mileage, but they are completed over days, sometimes weeks. A race of truth is completed in one concentrated effort, without any rest. The RAAM, in addition to being a race of truth, is 50% longer than "le Tour," and as a single stage race, it represents a distilled and sustained effort that is rarely seen in the world of sports.

"The Tour," as it is known in cycling circles, by comparison, is a stage race comprised of sections ranging in length. The general feeling from RAAM participants is not that The Tour is of lesser quality or importance, but rather that the RAAM is, mentally, a much more demanding race.

Another way of saying this is that the RAAM is not a race for wimps. The level of respect a cyclist can garner in cycling circles from participating in the RAAM verges dangerously close to the mystical. Tell any RAAM enthusiast that you've been a part of the most difficult race in the world and he's likely to get all misty-eyed and dreamy. The racers are viewed as being part of an elite family. It is, for some, the Holy Grail of the cycling world. It's also like Everest for climbers in that it doesn't really matter how many people have done it before; it doesn't really matter how long it takes to finish; it just matters that it was done.

The length of the race is a supreme challenge, and the riders aren't competing for giant jackpots. In fact, they aren't competing for any jackpots at all. There is no real prize for finishing the RAAM. There are no lucrative endorsements, no free handouts, no corporate handshakes or pats on the back. Instead, there is something almost unheard of in modern sportsmanship: the ability to relish finishing for the sake of finishing and earning bragging rights.

The race is pure because it resembles those halcyon days when sports were played for the sake of athleticism, for the fun of competition, and for the slim potential of a brief moment in the sun. "Finishers" in the RAAM, as they are called, are always "Finishers," a unique distinction shared by only a handful of individuals on the planet. This title is often the achievement of a life-long goal, and some have gone as far as to compare it to winning a medal in the Olympics. To attain a first place spot as a "Finisher" is without a doubt a feat guaranteeing a spot in the RAAM's version of the Hall of Fame, which includes a quick and cursory mention on the website as a "Top Finisher", not exactly the accolades one might anticipate for participating in and finishing what is arguably one of the most difficult races of any kind in the entire world. And so, with this in mind, some RAAM racers find some sort of sick condolence in the fact that their endurance of pain at a level that most people can scarcely imagine has potential for enshrinement in a virtual house of immortality and the knowledge that they finished. Again, any sane person might question whether any attempt at a race like this is worth it. Still, every year hundreds of enthusiasts make an attempt to finish.

The RAAM has a young history when compared with races like The Tour. At only twenty-seven years old (as of

2009), it lacks the formality of the more storied and fabled stage races around the world, though that may just be why so many cyclists attempt to compete in the RAAM. Perhaps the RAAM still provides the wiggle room to become a legend—at least within a small, cultish circle.

The Race is redolent of the ancient and venerable efforts of the forefathers of bicycle racing. At the turn of the last century, ambitious young cyclists met at velodromes, those large oval arenas where their spirits and physical abilities were tested on steeply banked tracks as they hurtled themselves along at what were—sometimes quite literally—breakneck speeds. Often these races went on for hours, even days, with thousands of laps being the norm rather than the exception. There are numerous accounts of turn of the century cyclists racing until they dropped dead on the banked velodrome tracks. Other stories tell of competitors who finished, only to find that their legs were so accustomed to the motion of cycling that they continued moving like some separate, autonomous, robotic entity for hours afterward. Some young men raced until, utterly exhausted, they fell asleep on their bicycles, careening off the track into throngs of thrilled onlookers.

People in those days placed bets to see who would collapse first—and last. The Race Across America, although not crowded with anxious onlookers, is like these early days of bicycle racing, when the sport of cycling was about pushing to the very frayed edges of human endurance.

RAAM racers have fallen asleep while riding. Serious injuries have been sustained by cyclists who have skidded off the road. Some have come to the brink of death, and others have died.

The Race Across America also follows in the footsteps of men like George Nellis, who in 1887 rode a High-Wheel bicycle clear across the expanse of the United States. At the time, well established roads were virtually non-existent. His trip took a crushingly enormous 88 days. He slept where he could—which frequently meant on the side of the rode—in ditches, and he ate what he could—a truly astronomical amount.

There is one story about his entering a grocer's shop advertising "all you can eat bananas." Nellis paid, ate, and continued to eat until he was asked to leave. One can only imagine the grocer's dismay at having such a business venture fail so unexpectedly. George Nellis's story is not the sole one about early crossings of the continent. There has, in fact, been a fairly long history of and fascination with crossing continents by bicycle. Most of these fantastical journeys focus on who has the ability to go faster or farther, and the RAAM is no exception to this rule. There is purity in the challenge that these types of races represent, and that essence is the driving force behind all adventurers, a fuse that once lit is all but impossible to extinguish.

Those who admire the RAAM frequently comment about it being a more honest race than many others around—including the Tour de France. It is, like I said, a "Race of Truth," a term which affectionately describes all types of races lacking multiple stages. The RAAM, unlike the Tour, has one continuous stage or leg, starting in California and ending in Maryland. In other words, when the clock starts ticking at the starting line it doesn't stop until the racers cross the finish line, over 3000 miles away. Often there is a gap of days rather than minutes or seconds between the teams on the leading edge and those that are last to cross the finish line. What all this amounts to is a race that has a distance of over 3000 miles (3021 miles in the 2009 RAAM) that must be covered as quickly as humanly possible, without any time for rest or recuperation. A handful of hours for sleep a day, say three or four, is considered luxurious. Most crew members and cyclists scrape by on a paltry two to three hours of sleep.

Teams in the RAAM move, in what must appear to the majority of passing motorists, as torpidly moving caravans across the country, stopping only when the necessity becomes absolute for fuel to power vehicles and bodies. The minds of cyclists and crew members get not a single rest. The competitive nature of the race, coupled with the mental expenditure of energy, leaves no room for daydreaming or meditation, especially when a wrong turn could cost, at the very least, loss of a cyclist's energy and motivation. In the worst case scenario, a wrong turn could lead to loss of life.

In order to be in the running for a coveted finishing spot a four-person team in the RAAM must complete the "course" in just under eight days. The fastest teams will make the entire trip in closer to six days. This is half the length of time that it takes competitors in the Tour de France to finish. During what is basically a week long period of time, racers on each team will climb the collected elevation of over 100,000 feet, pass through a total of fourteen states and crosses the five longest rivers in the United States: the Arkansas, the Ohio, the Mississippi, the Missouri, and the Rio Grande. The race is epic in every sense of the world.

There is also a solo division in the RAAM. The solo competition is a different animal entirely and perhaps better left as the subject of another book. Still, it warrants at least a brief mention.

Solo riders, the entire half-human lot of them, are legends

and lunatics in the minds of fellow RAAM racers. Soloists cross the country—a full continent I might remind you—in around nine days, stopping to sleep, produce bowel movements, and eat only when the natural inclination cannot be denied any further.

Soloists verge on the mythical. They are virtual machines, pumping legs in ceaseless rhythms—pow, pop, pow, pop. Some soloists have competed year after year, turning the race into a lifestyle.

It seems worthwhile to mention that the natural desire to sleep can be denied to a remarkable degree—longer than I ever thought possible and much longer than most people think. During the race all of the members of my team survived on approximately two to three hours of sleep a day for eight days straight.

I only hallucinated once. More on that later.

Still, sleep cannot be denied endlessly. Some racers have fallen asleep on their bikes, veering off the course into cacti, ditches, and in some cases—oncoming traffic. These same riders have picked themselves up, brushed the dirt out of their gashes, and continued racing.

Crew drivers are often no better. During the 2009 RAAM, one of the team members of team Surf USA, captained by Laird Hamilton, was struck from behind while riding his bicycle by the driver of a chase van, knocking him both literally and figuratively out of the race. This ain't a race for wimps. No way. No how.

Three

The night before leaving for the race was filled with the expectant tension that has come to define all of my travels. I paced back and forth, drank too much coffee, and ended up panicking in my search for a suitable bag. My wife watched patiently as I rolled socks and shirts, organized toiletries, and attempted to get things in order. I rummaged through the closet for about half an hour and pulled everything out from under the bed searching for a bag. Finally, I gave up and called my mother to see if she had anything that might work. The conversation went something like this:

"Mom, I'm leaving for my trip tomorrow."

"Oh, Kenny, I wish you good luck. Be safe and have fun."

"Mom, I'm calling because I need to see if I can borrow a bag."

"A bag?"

"Yes, a bag. A duffle bag. I need something small."

"Oh. I think I may have one. It's a tan, Ralph Lauren Polo. Will that work?"

"Yes. And Mom…"

"Yes Kenny?"

"You might never see it again."

Long pause. Silence.

"Oh. Well, come by and pick it up."

"Okay. I'll be there in a few minutes."

"Ok. Drive carefully. Bye-bye."

I got off the phone and drove at eighty miles per hour to my mother's house, fifteen minutes away. My first thought when I saw the Polo bag was, "Great. This should fit right in with the high-end, ridiculously expensive, waterproof North-Face Expedition stuff sacks that everyone else will no doubt have." I know this was immature in the most bovine way possible, but it's what I was thinking. Gear in the biking world and in the "outdoorsy" world in general is a big deal. I then drove back to my house, again at eighty miles per hour, and began the tedious process of packing the bag. Somewhere between cramming socks into the bottom and figuring out what to do with the powder for my feet, I got an unexpected phone call from Jim Bernard, the crew chief for our team, TeamSaveBuzzardsBay.Org.

It is a well-known and nearly universal rule of travel that there will always be last minute details that grow quickly to nightmarish proportions. The longer or more important a trip is, the more likely it is that some sort of cataclysmic event will occur the night before.

"Hey…Ken," began Jim's voice on the other end of the line. "We might have a small problem."

Here it was.

"Ken…do you have proof of your auto insurance?"

"What?"

"Auto insurance. Do you have proof of your auto insurance? The folks at RAAM Headquarters won't let anyone drive the chase vans following the bikes unless they have proof of auto insurance."

Shit.

Shit. Shit. Shit. Shit. Shit. Shit. Shit.

"Jim…I don't have it."

"It's okay," Jim reassured me, "I'm in the same boat. This is an easy fix."

An easy fix? We flew at 8:45 A.M. That was almost exactly twelve hours away. The insurance agency would, no doubt, be closed. And this was an easy fix.

"Yeah, I know man. Apparently the RAAM folks didn't let us know ahead of time that we needed to have proof of auto insurance for the trip, or, if they did, it wasn't communicated very clearly." Spoken like someone who has truly dropped the ball.

"Okay…so what should I do?"

"Alright, all you need to do is get proof of your insurance faxed to the Marriott in Oceanside before the race begins."

"Okay Jim. Will do. Bye." Piece of cake. No problem.

Smile outside, fume inside.

"Bye-bye." Just a tiny, isty bitsy bit of edginess.

I hung up the phone and thought about calling my insurance company, but figured that since they were closed, I'd only end up leaving a message and sounding like a lunatic. Then I sat around panicked for another half an hour until ten o'clock and decided to call anyway, because that's just how my brain works. Receive information—panic—think—act. Sometimes, actually most of the time, this works out. Don't ask me how, it just does. The insurance agent is a friend of my father, so I decided to call him directly. His answering machine picked up. I imagined him listening to my pathetic, tinny voice on his machine as he relaxed in his hot tub, sucking down a martini. I imagined the steam and mist rising up around him, enveloping him, his skin reddening, and his eyes wide as he laughed at my predicament.

"Ray. Mr. Gramlich. I...uh...need proof of my insurance. I mean for my car. I have to have it faxed to the Marriot Hotel in Oceanside, California as soon as possible. The fax number is..."

I went on, talking too fast, sounding like a lunatic, just as I had feared, for about two minutes. Then I hung up and prayed to the gods that help fools like me to do something to help out. My brain, still going at fifty-eight million miles an hour, fueled by caffeine, slowly, almost imperceptibly, came to a grinding halt.

Finally, I finished packing and slept.

Four

I woke in the morning at five, crammed some toast and coffee into my stomach, woke my wife and kids, and got going on my merry way. The moment before any journey is always the same for me. There is a sense of self-doubt, anxiety, and panic. These are the feelings that accompany each of my new adventures. Each new beginning and each movement away from what I know and what is to come is, to me, one of the most important parts of the trip. The beginning of the trip and the first step out the door represent the ability to move away from my present and towards some newer, unknown form of myself. I always want to become better as a result of my journey. My mind that morning was colored by all my previous experiences, and I stopped before walking out the door to drink it all in. Then, I walked on.

Five

A year before the race I didn't have even the slightest clue that I would've agreed to go on a race like this. But, like most things in life, one thing quickly leads to another. One year before the race I had just started a bicycle rickshaw business. I busted my rump pedaling rickshaws around the city of New Bedford, Massachusetts. I made nothing. And I mean nothing. People used to give decent tips, but the four cabs cost nearly $10,000. Once, I gave a four-hundred pound man a fifteen-minute tour—he gave me twenty bucks. All I got at the end of the season was in really good shape. At the time it was a total loss. I had invested ten grand in the rickshaws and thousands more in advertising and other miscellaneous things. I used to believe in the saying "If you can dream it, you can do it". Now I had a new mantra: "Hey, at least I tried."

Bills kept piling up and didn't show signs of stopping. At one low point I telephoned my financial advisor and, against his advice, took out a loan against my 403B. It became more and more difficult to make monthly payments on my mortgage. I was close to losing it all, including what little left I had of my reeling mind.

At the end of the season, when the weather began to turn cold, I needed to put the bikes in storage. I called Jim

LaBelle, the owner of a local bike shop, Village Bicycle, to see if he had any ideas. Jim and I didn't go very far back. In fact, the only reason I knew him at all was because he had helped me with fixing the rickshaws. He had agreed to maintain the bikes in exchange for advertising on the back of two cabs. In hindsight, I think he was really doing it just because he wanted to help out a fellow bike nut. There's a bizarre kind of camaraderie between bike enthusiasts.

I used to give him a ring on the phone about things that, owning a rickshaw business, I should have known how to do myself: fixing broken chainrings, changing flat tires, mending broken spokes. It was usually silly stuff— unimportant and tedious crap that I should've been able to fix myself.

The truth of the matter was that I didn't have the slightest notion about how to fix damn near anything on a bike. I couldn't even change a flat tire. Anyone attempting to open a bicycle rickshaw business should be able to do any basic repair work—blindfolded.

Jim used to repair things fast, well, and efficiently. I remember thinking: "Now, here's a man who can fix a bike." He'd ride his bike to come fix the rickshaws. It was, according to him, "a short ride". I got in my car to check the mileage after work one day and discovered that for Jim, "short" meant twelve miles, each way.

At one point during my business adventures one of my drivers managed to drop to chain off the bike and then continue pedaling, putting considerable pressure on the frame and chainring. By the time she was finished, somehow, almost inconceivably, she had managed to bend the frame completely out of shape, leaving it looking like some monster had decided to snack on it for lunch or pound its foot down on the frame just for the hell of it. Jim came down and looked at it, shaking his head in disbelief. Then, he turned his head slightly to the side, with that same puzzled expression that I would get to know so well, and said "Well...how do you suppose she could've done that?"

I hadn't a clue. Still, he managed to pick up the pedicab later that day on a trailer, bring it to his shop, and fix it with a frame puller of some sort. It was one of those things that was really far above and beyond what was considered part of our agreement. He had agreed on basic maintenance, not frame bending and metal fabrication.

Anyway, I contacted Jim about my storage issues and we discussed potential solutions for a few brief minutes before he consented to let me store them at his shop, over the entire winter, completely free of charge. It was one of the first times in my life that I had experienced such generosity.

In hindsight it was also one of the biggest paradoxes of personality in anyone that I had ever met. After the race there were to come such *accusations* of financial mismanagement and money pilfering that I could scarcely believe that Jim was the same person. Renting a storage unit for the four rickshaws for the winter would've cost me a bloody fortune. So, at the time, I felt blessed. The rickshaws, after a few faulty courtships, met a new and loving owner, but they sold for less than half of what I had originally paid for them. The sale left me with slightly over five-thousand dollars in loans to repay to various banks and angry credit card companies.

One day, after the sale of the bikes, I stopped by the bike shop to talk with Jim and to thank him. This was the moment that changed the course of event from tragedy to transcontinental trip. Jim was, as usual, very busy, but he took a couple of minutes to talk with me, and during the course of our conversation he told me, in a sort of off-hand way, that he was preparing for something called "The Race Across America".

He had actually called it the "RAAM". I hadn't heard of it, but it sounded great. I had been writing at the time for a variety of small, local magazines, and I was always on the lookout for a good story. I asked him if I could write an article for a local magazine about his journey. It really just seemed like one of those heartfelt, human-interest stories that people would eat right up.

That night I went home already thinking about weaseling my way into the race. I'm not even sure why I felt that way. I'm not normally one to insinuate myself into anything, never mind a transcontinental, very-expensive bike race. Nevertheless, my brain obsessed over the idea. I talked about it endlessly, until finally, my wife, totally sick of hearing me talk about it, said, "Why don't you just ask if you can go?"

A few days later, I was back at Jim's shop, in his office. It was early Spring and the grass was beginning to poke through the soil in thin needles of green. His desk was piled with bills and invoices; the walls were covered with posters of bicycles and bicycles themselves, hanging on hooks. Everything looked expensive and glittering. A stationary bike trainer was behind his desk with an extremely expensive bike perched on it. The computer on his desk hummed quietly away, and the phone kept ringing off the hook. Jim would, invariably, glance at the phone, check the number on the caller id, and simple say, "I'm not dealing with these people right now." He would then answer all of my questions I was asking for my itsy bitsy article for the local magazine. After about ten minutes it became clear to me that it would, in fact, be quite possible to write more than just a quick article about the race.

Six

There really is no telling what each adventure, each journey will bring. Sometimes it is unclear whether a journey will actually be of any importance whatsoever. It is my belief that only the vast potentiality that the journey represents is what is important—at least this is true at the journey's beginning.

Every person knows this feeling—this emotion—this movement towards chaos and the unknown at the beginning of a trip. It is a feeling that is at once unsettling and full of panic, a fleeting instance when, as travelers, we are able to most clearly grasp our potential for growth. Once the trip has begun, we are frequently so busy with the movement of the trip itself that we are unaware of what every moment might mean to us in the future. The panic of inception is in every beginning, and that is because what is to come is only a glimmering. It is the potential of any journey that is the most interesting. Then, there is the further realization that every single moment is like this, pregnant and full of potential.

Seven

I arrived at T.F. Green Airport in Providence at 6:05 A.M.

It was another hour before I made it through the various gates and checkpoints by taking off my shoes, shuffling through metal detectors, and getting frisked with wands. I made my way towards Gate 21 to catch flight 735, which would bring me from Providence to Baltimore. Then I would catch a connecting flight to Phoenix, where I would catch yet another flight to San Diego. The first flight departed at exactly 8:45 A.M.

Despite the fact that light jazzy elevator music was playing, the atmosphere at the airport quite quickly added to my general level of anxiety and tension. Every minute or two some sort of absurd anti-terrorism announcement came over the loudspeaker, informing me that "any and all bags left unattended will be collected and destroyed". Other speakers began announcing things like "Mr. and Mrs. John J. Dingle-heimer are going to miss their plane if they don't get their butts to Gate 80 in two seconds" and "Little Johnny Two-shoes is waiting for an escort at the main gate."

I began to hyper-focus on the announcements and all the other noises. A woman with two small children ran by, dropping her bag and swearing—"Holy Shit!" Then she

33

grabbed her children, rushing them towards the oblivion of the crowd. There was a palpable tension in the air—a combination of my own anxiety and the general and new fervor in the country that has defined the decade since the attacks of 9/11.

I did not deal well with any of these things.

People walked by, mumbling incoherencies about their flights, their delays, and their lost baggage. One man stopped, dropped his phone and continued to yell as it fell, "Those effers lost my bag! Dammit, dammit, dammit, we're going miss the effing flight!" He gave a cursory glance in my direction and seemed to sneer and snicker as he walked away. The tension in my body, made much worse by the cups of coffee I had just drunk, placed me on a razor's edge.

Then, it finally dawned on me why I was feeling this way; I was about to embark on a race that I really knew almost nothing about. I hadn't done any real research, I had no idea what to expect, and I knew only two people on the trip: Jim LaBelle, a man I really barely knew, and Chaney Becker, an acquaintance of mine from my prep school days back in Dartmouth, Massachusetts.

I reminded myself that I should relax.

I could hear my four-year old's voice in the back of my head, saying, "Dad. Dad. You've got to relax. You're getting really loud, Dad." He was always telling me things like this. He was always right. I did need to relax.

I started to repeat in my mind this crazy little mantra that I once read from Thich Nhat Han, the Zen philosopher. The mantra always worked, mostly because it made me think about how absurd it is for Zen philosophers to give advice to people with kids when they've never had to deal 24/7 with a child themselves. Still, what the hell, it worked.

"Breathing in, I calm my body, breathing out, I smile. Present moment, wonderful moment," I said to myself. For some reason this always made me laugh. I cracked a wide smile, laughed a bit too loudly, and then stopped myself. It was too damn late. The woman on my left got up and the man to my right glanced sidelong at me and inched perceptibly away. At that moment I became the lunatic that others avoided. I could've sworn that the man seated across from me began packing his bags up to leave the moment I laughed, the bastard.

I knew little about the RAAM and even less about what was coming. All I had done to prepare for the race was to read lots of book about the cycling world, not exactly the most thorough prep work I'd ever done for something.

Lance Armstrong's War was one of these books, a book about the dark, shaved underbelly of the cycling world—about doping, competition, bicycles as expensive as houses, the lunacy of cyclists' eating and sanitary habits—it had seemed like it might be particularly helpful at the time. I also read about Major Taylor, perhaps the first African American international sports superstar. I read about the history of the bicycle, about people who had traveled at a leisurely and sane pace across the United States. But I hadn't read a single page about the RAAM. Later, I would find that there are only a handful of books on the subject anyway.

As I sat there, I began to feel calmer from the Zen breathing exercises, foolish as it might sound. I began to think about my poor students, sitting in their uncomfortable chairs, sweltering in the heat of late June. I am an English teacher by profession, a writer by avocation. I had, miraculously, been granted time off, just a few days really, at the end of the school year—something nearly unheard of—to pursue this crazy dream, to write a book.

The thing that kept popping up in the back of my mind as I sat there was that not a single person I talked to knew anything about the RAAM. In fact, the most common response that I'd been getting over the past few weeks before I sat in the airport was, "You're writing about the what?" This filled me with a mixture of excitement, as in: "Hey, I'm writing about something that almost no one has written

36

about!" and trepidation, as in: "I'm writing about something that no one has written about…" It wasn't the best feeling I had ever had.

Eight

Months before the race began, before any of the crew members were even sure if we were really going to go on this trip, we had our first "official" meeting at the Bittersweet Tavern in Westport, Massachusetts. The atmosphere was relaxed with just a hint of that special something that accompanies first meetings between strangers. There was, at that point, a great deal of joy in the whole process, a feeling that we were all about to embark on something greater than ourselves. As I walked in, Jim LaBelle, rider and team leader, was separated from the rest of the riders. Later, after the race was finished, this separation would take on a more metaphorical meaning. But then, at the beginning, Jim seemed to float in some strange bubble of excitement and enthusiasm. He seemed unstoppable.

The other riders—Chris Lake, Tim Bryant, and Chaney Becker—were on the other side of the room. They sat there whispering to each other, sharing in the joy and camaraderie that only devotees of the same path could share, confident in their knowledge that each of them could cycle the pants off anyone else in the room. They sipped iced water, beads of moisture slipping down the sides of the glasses, shifted their muscular bodies in the seats, ready to ride.

We met that day to discuss the plan of attack, and in many ways it felt like a meeting that you might have before a battle. Our race organizer, Jim Bernard, lead us in the "The Plan." Jim was then, and still is, a high school biology teacher, something that became embarrassingly obvious when he accidently shushed us. He immediately apologized, to a round of laughter. He began with a PowerPoint of various scenic spots across the country. He gave us the initial impression that the race was going to be "fun" and that we would be able to take the time that we had "off" to go "sightseeing". This ended up being the furthest thing from the truth. To Bernard's credit, he wasn't aware of the hell that we were going to endure during the race. He was just as much in the dark as the rest of us about what the race was really about. And believe me, that's saying something.

The race, we would find out, was not about fun. No, I it wasn't really about fun at all. It was about supporting each other through mental and physical breakdowns, through tests, through trials we could not—at that moment—possibly comprehend. The race, we would quickly realize, placed us in a high pressure test chamber where we would be forced to explore the limits of sleep deprivation, mental fortitude and sheer will.

But at that moment—as we sat waiting for our

lunches to be served—we listened to the fantasy that Jim Bernard presented.

"There will be," he said, "3021 miles to cover in less than seven days." I sat pondering the idea for a minute, making a mental note to myself that the time period was, coincidentally, according to believers in Christianity, the same length of time that it took God to create everything. I chuckled to myself and reminded myself that we too might be resting on the seventh day, if I were to be lucky.

"This race is a cat," continued Jim Bernard, "it's a cat that can be skinned in about fifty different ways. We only have to choose one. Let's get Jim LaBelle up here to talk about the plan."

LaBelle, standing at 5'9" and 150 pounds, rose from his seat and walked, determinedly, to the front of the room. He had the physical stature and posture of a long time cyclist which, I later found out, was a souvenir of twenty-plus years of arching his back so that his hands could meet a pair of drop handlebars, known to cyclists as "the drops." There was, when he spoke, a convincing intensity and directness to his voice that was backed by his striking blue eyes. Everything he said seemed like fact—unquestionable and irreversible.

"We will," he began, "begin our race practice today.

We will go out after lunch and we will ride. We will make mistakes today, on purpose. We will make them now so we don't make them later. Or, if we do make them later, we will know how to deal with them."

Early on, when I had first discussed things about the race with Jim, he had expressed a similar sentiment by saying, "There are no problems. Only solutions. Solutions, solutions, solutions." We would find out that this, too, was not true. There are always problems. And on some occasions there are no solutions that are visible.

The race is something for which no amount of preparation can ever possibly be adequate. So, while we sat there, consciously consuming our food, laying white napkins on our laps, eating expensive foods, sipping, iced water from stemmed glasses, and all the while we had no idea of what we were headed towards, no idea that we would suffer, no idea that none of our preparations would really prepare us.

When lunch was finished we moved on, down the road a ways, to Village Bicycle, Jim LaBelle's business. He gave us specific instructions to be rude to his customers, which at the time seemed at odds with his usual Boy Scout demeanor. He told us, "We need to get in and out. Don't talk to anybody and don't say hello. The riders need to go in, get changed, and then we need to go." His directive was at the time—and unlike during the race—punctuated by a line of nodding heads and smiles of acquiescent silence.

We arrived at the bike shop after a three minute car ride. The clouds that were present earlier in the day had just begun to part and the blue sky had just become visible, considerably brightening both the landscape and the moods of the crew and the riders.

Bryant and LaBelle paced nervously in the parking lot, and there was a palpable tension in the air. It was the feeling of something big about to begin. It was the tension of money being spent. It was the tension of time passing and the tension of action about to unfold.

I remember thinking that the weather was perfect, and if it would hold, this would be a beautiful ride. I wondered at the time about what the weather would be like on the race.

Then I had glanced over again at LaBelle, Becker, Lake, and Bryant. They shifted uncomfortably in their cycling clothes, pulled at their crotches, adjusted their helmets endlessly. They looked incredibly nervous. Their apprehension probably stemmed from their major investment in this race. There was an enormous expenditure of both time and money spent in preparing for a race of this magnitude.

Part of the expense came from the sheer cost of

purchasing a good racing bike. Modern racing bikes have about as much resemblance to their predecessors as a MacBook Air has to a Smith Corona typewriter.

New racing bikes are light. And when I say light, I mean L-I-G-H-T. Each bike used during the race weighed approximately ten pounds. The bikes were machines designed for speed, and this speed came at a hefty price. Also, they were not the most comfortable bikes in the world. But, they were not built for comfort. The seats were wafer thin carbon fiber. Chris Lake affectionately dubbed them "nut crushers," and he emphasized that they were—in his words—"an acquired taste." At one point, about half-way through the race itself, he freely admitted to me that he would "probably be sterile" as a result of his affinity for using the bicycle as a device for genital torture. He said this with his affable smile plastered across his face, as if it were just par for the course. He was right, of course.

Carbon fiber is expensive stuff. The seat alone cost hundreds of dollars. In fact, it cost nearly as much as my lower-end Marin Larkspur city bike, which cost me $600 bucks new.

Pretty much every part of a modern racing bike is made of carbon-fiber, a sort of unique fabric and epoxy that is expensive to manufacture but one which every serious cyclists can't afford to be without. Simply put, to win races, a person needs a really, really light bike. And enormous strength.

But it is the carbon fiber that largely pushes the cost of bikes ever skyward. Chris Lake once told me that he was forced to make a difficult decision between buying a new car and buying his new carbon-fiber bike. He bought the bike.

His bike was, without a doubt, one of the most beautiful bikes I had ever seen, a ten-thousand dollar work of art made by legendary frame maker Parlee. Parlee frames represent a new level in the evolution of the bicycle. Each is meticulously handcrafted, polished, and caressed into something that begins to resemble a work of fine art— expensive fine art.

Then there were Tim Bryant's machines, bicycles that were not only custom built but custom fitted to his body.

Bryant, a Brit, stood out from the rest of the group, and not just because of his accent. At 220 pounds and 6 foot 2, he was a bit of an oddity in the realm of cycling, where a great number of athletes at this level weigh in at a rather scanty 150 pounds or so.

The first time I met Tim, I noted a deep and thoughtful intensity in his eyes, a mane of hair that rivaled that of his fellow Brit Percy Bysshe Shelley, and a physical stature that resembled that of a wealthy British aristocrat—shoulders back, back straight—with a walk and subtle grace that evoked privilege, power, wealth, and birthright. Tim was, according to LaBelle, a bit of a specialist, excelling at riding long distances on flat, or very nearly flat, roadways.

Tim's bulk and his riding specialty require unique, custom made—and therefore ludicrously expensive—bicycles. He had decided to bring both a road bike and a time trial bike on the trip. Time trial bikes are built to reduce drag, increase speed, and set records. They are light, more than slightly uncomfortable, can be as expensive as a typical used car, and are aerodynamic in nearly every conceivable way. The handlebars are not the typical "drop" style bars that have become standard on most racing bikes. Instead, time-trial bars are designed to be gripped in a straight forward position, so that the rider ends up with a hand position similar to that of praying. With the speeds that a rider can reach with these bikes, he may as well be praying. A spill at fifty or sixty miles per hour downhill may do more than send someone to the hospital; it may send him to an early grave. The basic goal of a time trial bike is the streamlining of the body so that air is directed away from the chest and neck and around the body. Traditionally a big chested cyclist is at a supreme disadvantage. Next time you see a professional level cyclist, pay attention to his chest, without staring, of course. Many of the top riders have freakily disproportionate bodies: giant legs and a thin chest. Time trial bikes are also designed with frames that are thinner and pedals that are slightly closer together than the average racing bike.

One of the most famous time trial bikes was designed for Lance Armstrong. It was known as the "Narrow Bike", a $250,000 Trek that ended up ill-fated and, ultimately, unused. Although, the statistics show that Lance was able to shave a considerable number of seconds off his time trial races. Apparently the bike was intolerably uncomfortable. Well, what's $250 grand to one of the world's top athletes?

Tim Bryant's time trial bike, although not even close to the price of Armstrong's, had the same basic goal. It was meant to help him with an extra edge of aerodynamics that would, hopefully, reduce his overall drag.

The two bikes, each custom built and polished and refined and fitted perfectly to Bryant's body, cost upwards of $15,000 dollars apiece. That was nearly $30,000 bucks worth of carbon fiber just for Tim's rear end alone, and since the other riders had one bike each, plus one set aside as a spare to be shared by all, it brought the grand total to nearly $50,000 to $70,000 dollars for all of the bikes on the trip.

Ridiculously impressive and dangerously insane, for a bunch of bikes.

Nine

Many of the crew took the same plane flight out to California. The flight attendant kept making jokes and saying "for real" after everything.

"In the very, very, very, very, very unlikely event that we will make water landing, your seat cushion can be used as a floatation device. This is unlikely because we are not passing over any real bodies of water, besides a few small rivers and swimming pools in people's backyards. For real…"

I always begin panicking when flight attendant start talking about things like this, and this time was no exception. He may as well have said, "In the unlikely event of a water landing, grab the seat cushion, jump out the window, and pray like hell that the cushion magically transforms into a boat to whisk you away back home." Or they may as well say, "Listen, if we crash, there's really nothing much you can do, so we've provided these seat cushions for you to muffle your screams or to absorb your excrement, because you'll all be shitting your pants by that point anyway."

Of course, I never gave any voice to these thoughts. I sat quietly, trying to look like I was contemplating the landscape or thinking about how wonderful the trip was going to be.

I tried my best to be all Zen about everything. That didn't work out so well. Instead I began to think about everything all at once, about how the race and the flight and my journey from home were all the same. I thought about the fact that—ultimately—I was moving in some sort of really bizarre circle, where my beginning was going to be my end and my goal. I had this strange realization as we sat there together on the airplane that we were all on this crazy adventure to move as far away from our comfort zones as possible and then to come back again to our homes. I realized that there was an emptiness and a darkness at the beginning of every journey and that it was this darkness that we all wanted to explore. We didn't know if the darkness was good or evil, whether it was an emptiness or fullness, a blankness or an area of perfect color. Maybe it was both—a paradoxical space or time both pregnant and barren simultaneously.

This is what I thought of when I tried to be Zen about it all, when I tried to chill out.

Then, we flew through the atmosphere at 600 plus miles per hour. We pushed closer to the edge of the darkness, hoping that we would be able to peer down and then be able to return home to tell about it.

Ten

We arrived in California and were promptly shuttled away from the airport by John Hesselbarth, the team photographer, and we proceeded to make our way to the hotel in Oceanside. On the way we stopped in Encinitas at a taco shop that boasted that they had the "Best Fish Tacos in Town". I can't say whether this claim was true because I opted out of that particular culinary delight, opting instead for the much safer "Best Bean Taco in Town." It was mediocre at best, something between sautéed flip-flop and broiled insole.

When we arrived at the Marriott in Oceanside, Chris Lake and Jim LaBelle were just pulling in to the parking lot on their bicycles. They still looked strong, happy, and unstoppable, which added considerably to our excitement. They were in the middle of a hundred-mile ride. LaBelle stopped and dismounted to help us check in, the cleats on his bike shoes clicking along the tiled floor of the hotel, giving him the strange appearance of some freshly shod animal. His legs were both muscular and spindly, every ounce of fat having been burned off of them. After a quick check-in he had headed back out, to finish the next fifty miles with Lake.

Upstairs we met up with Chaney Becker and Tim Bryant. They seemed relaxed, lounging around on the couches. Tim fiddled with his Blackberry, punching at buttons with his oversized fingers or talking to his office in New York, trying to sort out last minute details. Chaney seemed to stare into somewhere else, looking slightly amused, like some crazy guru, his hair upended, his gaze far-off and distant, as if he had already begun the race.

Later that day I had sat with Chaney in the foyer and chatted. He seemed concerned, preoccupied really, with what he was going to be eating. He asked me if I was capable of any culinary masterpieces and told me that I should come with him to the WholeFoods market to pick out supplies on the next day. I confided in him about the difficulties I was having paying my mortgage and the violent shooting near my home.

Two years before the race, my wife and I had been returning from a trip to the beach when we were witnesses to a terrible shooting. Thankfully, we were in our car. Sadly, our son was strapped in the back seat, so he became a witness to a violent shooting at the age of three. We had just rounded the corner to go home and we had seen a group of teens in front of us. They wore hooded sweatshirts and baggy pants. Essentially they looked like the stereotype of a "gangsta". Unexpectedly, one of them pulled a gun and fired into the glimmering afternoon light. There was no sound that I remember, only a body dropping to the ground without blood. They faced away from us into the darkness and emptiness of their souls. I jammed the car into reverse and pulled down a side street. I cannot remember clearly the next moments. I sped through red lights and down highways until I was as far away from that place as I could be. We ended up, strangely enough, at Chuckie Cheese's, trying to calm my son down, to distract him from the madness of the world.

As I spoke with Chaney, I thought about how one of my reasons for coming on this trip was to figure out what I should do next with my life. My family and I had witnessed a shooting, our house was worth 90,000 to 150,000 dollars less than we had paid for it, and we were miserable. We were worse than underwater, and the swift currents of what everyone was calling the "housing crisis" were drowning us in a deluge of Biblical proportions. The bank refused to assist us in refinancing, refused to talk, saying that we made "too much" on my hefty teacher's salary. This trip became, for me, a length of time to burn off the excesses of worry and fear that had wrapped around my life.

Fear controls and binds us with cords that chafe and cut, but if we are able to sever these cords and toss them into the fire, we are able to move forward. I needed, like so many other people going through the housing crisis, to gain the courage to walk away, to do the only thing I knew in my heart was right—to get my child and my family as far away from the city and its misery as possible.

Chaney had sat and he had listened. Finally, after a contemplative silence and a stare into the warmth of the California summer, he told me that I should leave the house. In his mellow, semi-surfer, semi-guru fashion, he murmured, "It's only money, man."

He was, of course, right.

When I got back home after the race, I turned away from the hell of the city and never looked back.

Eleven

Our first day ended with a pre-race dinner at a high-brow Italian restaurant called Rosia's, located a short walk across the parking lot from the Oceanside Marriott. I had thought that we might be out of place, wearing sporty bike clothes, sponsor T-shirts, and flip-flops, but no one seemed to care, not even in the slightest. Welcome to California.

I sat with Jim Labelle, Jim Bernard—our team's crew chief—along with Chris Lake to my right and with Andy Ferrarini, the medic, directly across. Up until the moment we sat down, I have to admit that many of the underlying tensions within the group hadn't yet surfaced. At least I hadn't noticed them. Of course, I am famously clueless when it comes to these things. It was during dinner that the ugly head of discontent began poking through. LaBelle ordered a plate of pasta heavy on the cream, with three different cheeses and sausage. The waitress, a middle-aged but attractive woman from Italy, smiled with her dark eyes and said, in heavily accented English, "I'll be surprised if you don't have a heart attack after eating this." We all laughed, albeit a bit nervously. It seemed such an ironic thing to say to a man who had been training for the race of a lifetime, a race that had taken over a year of training to prepare for, who probably had the strongest heart of anyone in the restaurant.

LaBelle turned back to the table to stare intensely at his glass of water. He had a far off look in his eyes, as if something was eating at him. Part of this tension, I would later learn, was from a deep anxiety about finances, a distrust of Tim Bryant (unfounded, from what I gathered), and a struggle for, somewhat classically, power in decision making during the processes of both preparing for and racing the race.

At the time I had questioned whether it was just my imagination or some other trick of the light casting shadows over the whole scene. As I had glanced around the table, it seemed that others, particularly the racers, had similar glassy stares.

I suspected that some of them were on the race for reasons other than just proving that they could pedal across the country. I suspected that they were out to conquer some inner demon. There is, of course, no way of telling if this is true from looking someone in the eyes. People are always so damn tight-lipped about these things, these matters of the heart. The false face doth hide, or so our buddy Shakespeare wrote.

LaBelle's tensions had manifested themselves in odd ways—mostly in his predilection for cleanliness. He was opening doors with his sleeves, washing his hands with waterfalls of hand sanitizer, wiping his silverware before eating—the whole nine yards.

LaBelle's penchant for sanitization of his body and his environment prompted Andy Ferrarini, our team medic, to say, "It's just getting way too easy to make fun of you, Jim."

Jim looked back at Andy and said, "You know, it's because I'm worried. I'm not just worried a little bit. I'm worried a shitload." At the time it wasn't clear whether Jim's anxiety was about cleanliness or about the race itself, but either way, it drew another bout of nervous laughter from all of us.

Jim Bernard, riding the wave of this humor, said, "I have something to say. I'd like to paraphrase the comic Steven Wright, who once said, 'It's a small world, but I wouldn't want to paint it.' Well, I say, it's a small world, but I wouldn't want to ride across one of its continents by bike." Har, har. Lots more laughter ensued.

The only thing was that The Race Across America is no joke, not even by the longest shot you could make. People during the race routinely bring themselves to the edge of mental and physical collapse, on purpose, just to see how much they can stand. Imagine running seven back to back marathons and you might just start to get a bit of an idea

56

about the intensity of this race. Imagine saddle sores that never go away, endless thirst and hunger. Imagine virtually no sleep. Imagine staring into the abyss. This is what we were about to embark on. So, while the laughter rang around the room and gradually subsided, there came a sense of unease about the entire operation on which we were about to embark. At times like these it has become customary for a leader to arise from the ranks of the mildly bemused and slightly confused in order to make some sense of the various parts of the equation, to put things back into some sense of order. To do this well, to rally the troops, a leader must have a great deal of either intelligence or charisma. The best leaders have both. The weakest have only the latter. The words from the team leader should lend inspiration where there was none, leading the poor souls who have lent their time and potentially risked their lives, to a cause that they are hoping will give them a taste of adventure, a glimmer of what it must be like to be either eighteen again or immortal, or that they are hoping will help them to escape the mundane existence of their everyday lives.

In this case, Jim LaBelle rose to the occasion to give perspective on things. Jim LaBelle, who against the advice of Jim Bernard—the team's crew chief—travelled across the country with the RV and the two minivans a week before the race was to begin in order to transport the bikes and to get things ready. During this escapade just days before the race, LaBelle logged an impressive driving stint in excess of 1200 miles at a single, sustained whack, stopping only for a quick refueling, and, as I later surmised, hardly at all to pee. Why stop when you can use a bottle, right?

LaBelle's pep-talk began with a brief recounting of his transcontinental journey by RV and minivan, saying that it, "Gave a lot of perspective. I realized that this country is so big, and that this is a big, big race, and that I'm going to have to take it slowly. At least more slowly than I might think I have to. If I can go at eighteen miles per hour, I should go sixteen." These words would return to plague our team in the early stages of the race. It is, of course, a unique tendency of all humans, it seems, to have a sincere inability to stick to plans, especially when the plans need sticking to the most.

Jim's speech continued on, and it was mostly short and mostly sweet, overflowing with the typical honey which flows from the mouths of men during these occasions. We were, for the moment, still inspired, still full of hope.

Twelve

June 18th, 2009

Pre-Race Preparations

The race was scheduled to begin at 2:00 PM sharp on June 20th. We were busy two days before, getting the wheels of our enormous race machine in full motion. Packing bags, polishing bikes, adding last minute details to last minute lists, and trying to make the whole affair look effortless.

Already there was a problem with our collective lack of sleep. Mostly this was because we were all suffering from jet-lag. There's a three-hour time difference between Providence, RI and Oceanside, CA, so all of us who decided to fly in started the race with minds that resembled partially melted sticks of butter. Since I had arrived in California, I was getting up at 2:00 AM, 4:00 AM, and finally and fully up at 5:00. It was fitful sleep, barely adequate for getting "rested up" before a big race. I felt at the time that I would be able to manage, particularly since I have borne the difficulties of seeing two children through infancy and all the accompanying sleeplessness that that entails. But I was to find out that I was slightly mistaken. Nothing can prepare someone for the type of sleeplessness associated with a race of this sort.

I watched from the living room of the hotel as Ed, Jim

Bernard, and Craig Mace shuffled out of the bedrooms, grabbed cups of coffee, took showers, and generally prepared for the day ahead.

Once we gathered the entire team and ate a light breakfast we all drove down to the Pacific Ocean with the minivans to pick up light bars, big flashing lights for the tops of the minivans. The ocean was bright, startlingly blue and there was an enormous pier with cement pilings and a boardwalk on top. The pier extended several hundred feet into the Pacific. Andy couldn't resist the call of the water. He ran down and soaked his feet for a few minutes while we waited. We had about a half an hour to spare before we needed to check in with the RAAM folks, so we spent some time walking around the waterside and then down along the pier. A large Coast Guard helicopter hovered nearby while we walked, sending ocean spray high into the air. It looked as though they were doing some sort of training exercise. We passed by a large number of Mexican immigrants who fished off the pier with incredibly large fishing poles. They had buckets nearly overflowing with fish. Finally, we made our way over to the RAAM headquarters.

Truly, the RAAM headquarters looked like a family affair. There was a small office which consisted of an awning set up to block the sun. RAAM officials stood at small tables selling books about ultra-marathon cycling, dvds of former races, t-shirts for loved ones back home, hats with logos, and other souvenirs. I stopped at the table and bought a bright red RAAM hat for twenty bucks and a children's book, starring Geronimo Stilton the mouse, for my four year old son. In the book Geronimo Stilton, a mouse with an affinity for good cheese, gets *tricked* into competing in his own Race Across America. In hindsight, it is clear why he had to be *tricked*. I figured at the time that it might just help my son figure out why I was gone for so long. I had told him that I was following bikes, but he really had very little notion of what I was doing. He just knew I was gone for a while. I have to admit that at the beginning of the race I began to wonder that myself.

I began to wonder why we, as humans, choose to do things like this race. The adventuring spirit is often misunderstood, not only by others, but by adventurous spirits themselves. Many of the people on the trip with me seemed to feel the same way. In addition, people in my family couldn't really understand why I would want to do something like this. Some seemed angry, some were confused, and none of them really asked me about the trip or asked me why I was doing it. They didn't ask why it was so important to me. Maybe they didn't care. Maybe they shouldn't have. I began, slowly, to realize that I really didn't know why I went either. I wasn't even sure I cared myself. But I also began to realize that I was there to find out what makes my type of people tick. I wanted to find out, not only why other people had decided to come on this trip but why I had decided to come—why I had decided to enter this unknown territory.

Thirteen

People often nearly die during the RAAM.

Two people have died during the race.

This is not something, that for obvious reasons, is widely advertised.

Why would anyone want to go on a race where he might die?

Even before the end of the first day spent preparing for the race, I knew that my initial ideas about how I would write about the subject just wouldn't work.

I had this whole grandiose idea that I would focus solely on the racers. I thought that they were probably in this race for one or more of a *laundry list of reasons* I had prematurely invented in my mind.

I thought that I would be able to write a play-by-play of all the events on the trip.

My list looked something like this:

LIST OF PROBABLE REASONS A PERSON WOULD WANT TO COMPETE IN THE RAAM:

1. To prove that he can.
2. To conquer some inner demon.
3. He/ she lost a bet.
4. To prove the perseverance of the human spirit.
5. Narcissism.
6. Eccentricity.
7. Pure athletic challenge.
8. He only has a year or two to live.
9. To say "eff you" to a dad that was never around.
10. He is insane. *(My personal favorite.)*

Within the first day, I began to think that this list was partial, flawed, and insufficient. By the end of the trip I recognized that the list was not only accurate, but that nearly everything on the list applied not only to the racers but also to me.

The observations about the race, I realized, would have to be not only about the racers but about the human spirit, the psychology of the race, and the psychology—and sometimes psychosis—of an adventurer. Finally, that last day before the race proper was to begin, I had a brief moment of clarity in which I realized that I had been thinking of myself as separate, as a completely objective observer of the events that were going on around me. I wanted to be detached, journalistic, and full of objectivity. Then, suddenly, I knew this attitude and approach couldn't be maintained.

I had made the choice to fly over three-thousand miles to California to make what many consider an insane journey in an equally insane bike race that the average American would probably look at as an act of complete lunacy.

The RAAM has no big money prize. It has no monetary prize at all. To "crew" the RAAM, a person must agree to give up between 8 and 14 days of his life, function on around two hours of sleep per day for eight days straight, and emerge a fragile husk at the end of it all. Many people, even if they were getting paid, wouldn't conceive of such a thing.

We were all choosing to do it for zilch, zippo, nada.

I was one of these people.

What the hell were we doing there?

This became my biggest and most fundamental question as the race began. It lurked and crept through the back of my mind, twisting itself into strange shapes, making it impossible for me to mold any answers. I can only guess that this is the type of questions that goes through the minds of anyone embarking on a major expedition, and the RAAM really is more like an expedition than a bike race. Tim Bryant, gave the Race a nickname: "The Traveling Carnival of Fun and Pain". The folks who promote the RAAM compare it to climbing Mount Everest.

I've never climbed Everest, but I can bet that members on the crew of a major Everest expedition must have felt the same things we felt at the beginning of their trip. Mostly though, I'll bet that they looked up at the vastness of the mountain and said, "Wow! That's really beautiful! Now, what the hell are we doing here, again?" A few of them probably wished that they could just go home, curl op on the couch, and fall asleep to old reruns of "I Love Lucy". Others, I'm sure, like most of us, felt that they should go on, that they were somehow duty bound like those that went before them. I felt like those early British explorers who carried copies of Shakespeare with them, thinking the whole time, "This is going to be jolly good fun, isn't it?"

I wasn't separate from any of the people on the race. I was firmly one of them.

Fourteen

Later in the first day of preparations, we drove down in the RV to a parking lot to get our team's equipment and vehicles inspected. There we met Lanie Smith, one of the many volunteer organizers of the race. He looked like a skinny old hippie, typical of California. He wore some RAAM clothing, a RAAM baseball hat, glasses, a shortly cropped beard and a long grey ponytail. He looked, quite frankly, nothing like what I expected a race organizer to look like. I had expected raw power, perhaps a retired racer, maybe a muscle-bound powerhouse of speed. Instead, there was Lanie. We started talking and I realized just how wrong first impressions can sometimes be. He had a look of killer determination in his eyes and a hearty laugh to match. We introduced ourselves as a rookie team and he was kind enough to give us a few words of advice from his own RAAM experiences. In contrast to his somewhat scrawny exterior, Lanie had personally ridden the RAAM twice, crewed it four times, and officiated it ten times. He spouted of the numbers as if they were as familiar to him as the alphabet. I was floored. Just riding in the RAAM is an impressive feat; having ridden it twice is an astonishing act of pure will. I was quick to notice that Lanie also had an almost surreal quietness to his demeanor. This seemed to be true of nearly all the veteran racers that I had met, especially so for those who had raced more than once.

These folks were a different breed. They seemed hearty, full of laughter and life, but then they'd turn quiet all of a sudden, thoughtful and contemplative. I didn't really know what to make of their silence at the time. Now I know in my heart that it is a result of touching a part of consciousness and will power that few people ever access.

After chatting with Lanie, we walked over to a rented, bright yellow Ryder truck where the light bars were being stored. Right away it was apparent that there had been some sort of clerical mix-up. Our team wasn't on the list for any light bars, a necessity for racing and a requirement of competing.

During the race lights are essential. A team can opt for the placement of small, breast-shaped lights on the back of each van—the kind that are seen in 1970's films where the cops pull magnetic lights out of the glove box of an undercover Chevy Nova, slapping them on the roof. They always look so impressive when they're first placed up on top, but halfway through the chase scene they are, inevitably, knocked off, and end up hanging over the hood and flying off around when the protagonist wheels around an impossibly sharp turn. The race officials discourage using this type of light, but in a friendly, later we will say "we told you so" kind of way. So, as an alternative, they rent light bars.

The light bars are fancy looking versions of the same concept. They are custom made. They are heavy. They are ugly. They are also bright yellow and sit on the top of the support vehicle, in our case a Toyota minivan, making the entire caravan on RV, minivan, and cyclist look like something out of a Mad Max film. The only difference is that the light bars, instead of being matte black primer in color, are painted bright, shiny, sunny, obnoxious yellow and have fancy little brackets on each side to hold two extra bicycle wheels. When the light bar is finally placed atop the caravan's roof, the whole contraption ends up looking like some bizarre clown car accessory crossed with a lame attempt at highway safety. These light bars serve another purpose besides that on providing vehicle safety. They also provide race team identification via an assigned number that is affixed to the light bar.

When following the riders during the race, the chase vans have to match speed and adjust as necessary. If the racer goes fifteen miles per hour, the van goes—you guessed it—fifteen miles per hour. This makes for some dangerous driving. To get a good idea of the dangers it might be helpful to imagine yourself driving down the highway. Now imagine that you are cruising along at, say, a comfortable seventy miles per hour. Now, imagine that you get behind a guy who's going fifty. Now suddenly reduce his speed to fifteen miles per hour, throw a cyclist on an expensive bike fifteen feet in front of him, have the road change unexpectedly into a narrow, barely passable one lane, add lots of bumps, potholes, 110 degree weather, steep 15% grade, hairpin turns, a few broken beer bottles, several discarded semi-truck tires, and a handful of extend middle fingers. Now, attempt to pass this cyclist and chase van. Just as you are about to pass a semi hauling tandem trailers races towards you at eighty miles per hour. Now, that will give you just a wee taste of why the officials want people to use the biggest, ugliest light bar contraption that anyone could ever design. They just want people to get noticed.

We soon learned that Bob O'Connor was the race official who dealt with light bar distribution. He was the master of the light bars. He double-checked his list. Then he told us that we were only down for one light bar. We needed two. Jim Bernard, our fearless crew chief, with his Marine Corp. background, didn't skip a beat. "There must be a way we can get an extra, right?" Bob, who had the general straightforward manner that I have come to associate with former military men smiled and said, "I'll check," and "surer-n'shit" he pulled one out and some of our boys mounted it up on the roof. As we were walking away I looked back at Bob, and I saw a little glint in his eye. It wouldn't surprise me at all if I found out someday that he was a RAAM veteran too. There's a whole family cult atmosphere about the race.

Fifteen

We sauntered over to the main team check in center later that day, where we met Rick Boethling and his mother Gayle. Both supremely welcoming people, they lead us to a small, rather makeshift looking "central office," where the official check in process had been refined over the years to something akin to a science. These two are a RAAM institution. Some might even say that they are the RAAM, that without them it would crumble. We learned that Rick's dad, Fred Boethling, held the RAAM record for the over sixty division until just recently, when it was shattered. Gayle told us, with a somewhat worried and pained expression on her face, that he felt that he really needed to defend his title, but that there was no way that she was "willing to go through with that all again." It seemed clear that what she really wanted to say was that she was unwilling to go through with all the loss of time, the pain, the suffering, and the tension that is involved with the race. It would've just been too much to deal with. I asked Rick if he had an intention of doing the race. He said that he really didn't intend to, but that with a little bit of prodding he might, just might, entertain the idea of another race, especially if it was something that he could do with his dad as a two-person team, or as a four person family team. Rick also told us about some of the slightly insane food requirements of the riders. Andy Ferrarini, the team medic, got slightly excited at hearing the mention of food, immediately asking about the famed and fabled "Navajo Burrito," a human head sized Mexican delight that has achieved folklore status among RAAM racers and crews. According to many veteran racers I spoke with, racers have single-handedly downed the "Navajo Burrito" in a single sitting.

This is not tremendously surprising, considering the fact that racers consume enough food to raise their daily caloric intake to just around 9,000 calories—give or take a few. The burritos, we were told, were located in Tuba City, in the heart of Navajo Territory. I made a mental note to get one and try it, but by that point in the race I was too sleep deprived to remember my name, never mind a burrito.

As I stood there listening to Rick I started to think again about what we were headed for, out into the deep and great unknown. My best guess at that point was that whatever was going to happen to us would happen with or without our consent. This journey was about to take us into the deepest recesses of the human mind, past the places of mundane predictability, past all semblance of order, and into the passions of our senses. We were about to enter that weirdish, wild, dark and black emptiness of the future. We were scarcely able, at that moment, to comprehend what we were doing, never mind what we were about to do.

Rick pulled me out of my reverie by telling us we had to move over to a parking lot down the street, for a 1:45 inspection. This is when things started to really get moving. It was this moment that I finally had to admit to myself that we were going to be leaving soon. We needed to take mental stock of where we were headed and what we were about to embark on. We needed to begin.

Waiting around for a race to begin for several days is enough to drive anyone insane. It was even starting to drive wedges between members of the team. People were starting to get on each other's nerves. LaBelle and Bryant had already started to have hushed and muffled arguments about finances and strategies, though I was not privy to the information.

We picked up our rag-tag group and drove down to a beachside parking lot a short stretch up the road. Girls with impossibly small bikinis strolled past, and the sun baked the blacktop until, unable to absorb any more heat, it released invisible plumes of hot air that surrounded us. We sweltered and suffered. Everything came with us for the inspection. And I mean everything: the RV, two minivans, bikes, equipment, coolers, bike stands, tools, stickers, medical supplies, racers and crew members.

Each cyclist in the race is required to have two helmets, shoes, and a jersey with a RAAM patch in the upper left shoulder. The inspection proceeded in an almost militant perfection, with exhaustive checklists of how a team does or does not comply with official standards of the RAAM. Vehicles, lighting systems for the bikes, and the kind and type of tires, helmets, pedals, shoes—nearly anything you can think of—must accurately fit the race organizer's definition of acceptable and comply with their strict and high standards. Rules ruled in that parking lot. If even one thing was out of place—no race.

Needless to say, teams are panicked about getting everything "just right" the first time.

Each bike is subjected to especially close scrutiny. Besides being a mean, lean racing machine, and in addition to having the bare basics of all safe bikes—brakes that will work when squeezed, gears that will shift without grinding to pieces, both a headlight and taillight—each bike must also be fitted and modified to fit the RAAM requirements in other ways. Reflective tape, for instance, must be applied to the frame of the bike, to the rims of the wheels, and even to the spokes so that the bike maintains a unique "light signature" during the race. The term "light signature" refers to the unique appearance of any given reflective or self-illuminated object at night. The more that the light that is reflected from a bicycle looks like, well, a bicycle, the better the light signature is considered. The wheels, ideally, should look like rings of light when the bicycle is in motion. The pedals should look like bits of light pumping up and down in an alternating fashion. Creating a unique light signature is safe but aesthetically displeasing. The shame of the whole thing when it comes to beauty is that these bikes, left alone are beautiful works of art. When the bikes that the cyclists push along cost nearly ten-thousand dollars and look like finely polished works of museum worthy art, the last thing a person would consider doing is covering the whole thing with industrial strength, adhesive backed, reflective sticky tape. Yet, that's exactly what the RAAM officials require.

This obsession with reflectivity is in the spirit of safety, and I can attest that the well-being of the riders is, indeed, improved vastly with the application of this tape. But what a damn shame about the looks of the bikes.

Sixteen

The temperature in Southern California always seems to hover just around 80 degrees, with a slight breeze and not a cloud in the sky. One store I went in even had the weekly forecast permanently painted on the wall. Sunday, Monday, Tuesday, Wednesday, Thursday, and Friday all had the same outlook: Sunny, 85 degrees, beautiful. This is Southern California. This is the land of perfection. This is the land where everyone is friendly and no one is stressed out. Every corner on every street has a coffee shop or a surf shop, a bodybuilder or a blonde bombshell, an aging hippie in an old VW bus or a businessman in a Lotus Esprit.

Then, in the middle of it all, someone decided to start the RAAM.

Why, I'll never know.

Then again, it is California.

Seventeen

I rode back to the hotel after the inspection in the RV. Andy had put on some Credence Clearwater Revival. John Fogerty belted out "I wanna know…have you ever seeeeeeen the rain…" while Jim LaBelle lay on the sofa punching keys on his Blackberry. Eavesdropping shamelessly, I heard him talking to his wife about his daughter. She was sick. He asked his wife to put his daughter on the phone and then I heard him say, "God Bless Your Dreams." Then it was goodbye. This was one of those moments that made me think about how much effort and support went into a race like this. Each of us on the trip considered why we were there, but we should also have been considering all of the various people who helped us in attaining our dreams. It was at that moment, when I listened in on Jim's conversation, that I realized that it was not just me that was making this dream happen.

In every adventure there is something larger than and much bigger than a crew of people jaunting off around the world. There is something that is as large as we will allow ourselves to admit. Every adventure of this magnitude requires the support of a tremendous number of people: wives, children, parents, and sometimes even an entire community.

If we are to step back a few paces and fully consider the magnitude of our journey's impact, we would have to include all of the people who have supported us on this trip as well as all of the other people who support them while we are gone. There is an endless chain of humanity that supports each member.

While I was mulling over these ideas, we pulled into the parking lot at the Marriott. After Andy parked I got a chance to chill in the RV with Tim Bryant, who sat with an unusually contemplative air hanging around him. Tim told me that he had only been riding with Jim LaBelle for about three months when Jim had approached him about riding in the race. Tim felt that if Jim had wanted him to do it, he should give it a try. Bryant is a renaissance man. He's really one of those people who's a bit larger than life. Other people tended to view him as a bit of a pain in the ass, but I never got that impression from him. They may have felt that way because, as Ellen McNally, our team chiropractor said, he was "wealthy, powerful, and of high status." Wealth and power can make people jealous. Plus, Bryant is a man used to giving directions not taking them.

The animosity towards Bryant during the race, from the very beginning, made me wonder how much of our understanding of others is actually based on who we are inside and what we have experienced. Our ideas about others really has so much to do with perception and very little to do with reality. We shouldn't even bother to concern ourselves with the perceptions of others, as they can often be entirely inaccurate assessments of who we are. I realized then, as I do now, that we must deeply consider the perception of others as being a direct result of their minds and not so much a true understanding of the reality that surrounds them.

Tim speculated that the race was, for him, about much more than the opportunity to race. Like me, he had come for something else, something much larger. He was the most well-spoken man on the team. His words were refined, weighted, polished, and spoken like a man who is in full command of his mind. His reason for going on the trip bordered on the spiritual, though, as he said, "perhaps spirit isn't the right word." I found this endearing, for I've never been sure about the word "spirit" either. To say that the race is some sort of spirit quest implied a sense of knowing what a "spirit" is, and I wasn't sure that any human is ever really qualified to say exactly what a "spirit" is. It could be the center of our being, the seat of consciousness, or a biological apparition that we project from some bizarre mixture of chemicals in our minds. I had the feeling that Tim felt the same way. He was then, and still is, a successful architect, the operator of a well-known and respected business. He holds a formidable frame, bearing himself in a noble manner, stoic yet responsive, maybe even sensitive. He compared the race to a Hertzog movie, saying that the race to him was a sort of amateur racer carnival, an event uniquely and peculiarly American, full of the potential to provide something in our lives that we would get nowhere else. Interestingly, whatever we were about to get from this race, he didn't want his clients to know much about it. He told me that he had left the space for racer's occupation in the official information form for the RAAM blank—he feared that his clients, some of them rather high profile individuals, might think he was a lunatic.

One of these clients is the CEO of Walt Disney. I had to admit that the race was extreme, and a CEO of a powerful corporation might think twice about hiring an architect who decided to race across the country with a herd of loons. Tim's eyes are bright, enthusiastic, full of passion, full of life, but also filled with a desire to achieve something, prove something. As we sat there in the RV, with the early summer air blowing through the open door, with the California sun blazing overhead, Tim told me something that I had already thought myself, that this race was about community, camaraderie. It was and still is for me, about something beyond the race. It was about friendship and about finding out what we were made of. It was about figuring out how all of our understandings about ourselves are colored by our minds. It was about seeing the world clearly, burning off the fat, and seeing what remains. It was about attaining objectivity. It was, ultimately, about enlightenment. And, maybe, just maybe, it was about a bunch of us having what amounts to a collective mid-life crisis.

For some of the racers it was about conquering. For LaBelle, it seemed to be about conquering something within himself, perhaps becoming the great athlete that he had always wanted to be. LaBelle had always wanted to be either an Olympian or a racer in the RAAM. His dream was about to come true. Chaney Becker was a mellow surfer dude, but he had something to conquer too, a goal, and an unstoppable drive to achieve it. For Chris Lake, the whole race appeared to be a casual affair, something that he had just decided to do for a new and fun experience, just as someone might decide to go for a short walk down to the beach. But for Tim, there was something more, and really, when it comes right down to it, this goal was to reach a communion of sorts between mind, body, and other humans that, according to Tim, "can only be found in war, and I don't want to go to war." His comment had reminded me of those great Hemingway novels, For Whom the Bell Tolls and A Farewell to Arms, where the characters are fully alive only when tested to their extreme limits, sometimes even to the edge of death. There is something so beautiful and sad about living. Tragedy and comedy I suppose. Call it whatever you like, but we're all in it together. We are most electrically alive when we test ourselves to the limit, and in some sense this is sad. But when we test ourselves to the ends of our endurance, life is really quite beautiful, for it is in those moments that we experience the fullness of life with the most profundity. It's a beautiful paradox. John Donne and the metaphysical poets would've been quite proud. The Carpe Diem poets would've too, if they hadn't been so busy thinking about sex.

There are times when all we do is work, and Tim and I discussed how this was probably part of the problem that keeps us from ourselves, keeps us from becoming more fully human. To him, a lack of success in life is only due to a "failure of the imagination," which causes most people to lack the drive and the motivation to do much of anything at all. At the time of the race, Tim had two young boys at home, one three years old and the other two. His wife, he said, "probably vacillates between cheering him on and despising him" for his choice to race. There was definitely the general sense of the existential crisis in all of our discussions. Tim had even called an attorney earlier in the day to work on his Last Will and Testament. I couldn't decide at the time if this action was troubling or reassuring. It is a strange thing to confront a man facing the possibility of his own death, considering his own mortality, worried about the possibility that his considerable talents and wealth might get squandered, that his family might be without a father. Tim told me that his own father was hardly ever around, that he had had to grow up largely on his own, that he turned early in life to the poets of British literature, people who embraced the imagination, people like William Wordsworth, Blake, Keats. These were people who lived in the spots of condensed time that pull us all forwards into the greatness that we are all, perhaps, capable of achieving. Tim had come to America when he was twenty-one, with a passion. He impressed me that day in the back of the RV that he was a man on a spirit quest, a traveler, a man capable of anything, like us all, on a great and epic journey that we call life.

Eighteen

Later that same day, after retightening the light bars and tidying up the vans a bit, organizing coolers and bottles of water and the like, we all went back to the hotel. I went up to the room to get a little rest and ended up talking with Ed Zabilski. Ed was a somewhat enigmatic character, and he had come on the trip, like many of us, after a sort of chance encounter with Jim LaBelle's enthusiasm. Jim, after months of hard training, had begun to go to both a chiropractor and a massage therapist for much needed manipulation of his spine and muscles. Ed was his massage therapist, a tall, somewhat stoic man with twinkling blue eyes and a fully developed mustache.

I immediately liked Ed because he was quiet, thoughtful, and contemplative even. I lay down on the couch and we started talking about how he came to find himself on this journey. To my initial surprise, he told me that within five minutes of working on LaBelle's tightened back he was being asked to go on the race. Jim had just up and asked him if he wanted to go on the trip. There was no elaborate explanation, no detailed questioning of qualifications. Ed said that it was as if Jim wanted an answer right then and there. Jim's like that. Once he makes a decision, he sticks with it. He makes decisions quickly, and he expects others to be able to do the same thing. Well, Ed went. Ed also said that most of the cyclists had major issues with their bodies from so much exercise. He told me that their major problems related to their neck extensors, wrist flexors, quadriceps, hamstrings, and calves. To me that sounded like just about every part of a body that shouldn't be in pain. The relatively unmentionable pain of sitting on a carbon fiber bike seat for thousands of riding miles isn't something that Ed mentioned. Then again, that's not exactly his area of business.

Ed testified to Jim's endurance for pain, something that all ultra-marathon athletes must develop. "He never complains about pressure. I'll see him wince sometimes, but he always says, 'Just do what you need to do. Don't worry man; just do what you need to do.' It's actually really amazing, he's not going to let me know, to show any hint of weakness." All of the riders had this same attitude. It was both a testament to their mental and moral fiber and a sign of their unwillingness to lose. All athletes at this level have it, that quality of absolutely unremitting power to endure pain and to hide their pain from the competition. It is probably that same pairing that makes many of the riders successful in so many other areas of their lives. It is only after a race that these guys will say how they feel, when the pressure to win is off. I talked to John Asselin, the team's mechanic about this and he said that, "Days, sometimes weeks, later, Jim will tell me, 'Ed beat the shit outta me, man.' Or 'I was worried as hell about that race.'"

Nineteen

Celebrity never seems very far away in California. While driving back towards the hotel in the beastly RV, we saw former Patriot's quarterback Junior Seau grabbing an icy beverage at the local corner store. I was then and still am unusually unimpressed by celebrity, though I've got to admit that I'm not sure if that's because I've trained myself to be this way or if it is a genuine distaste. Perhaps I don't fully understand wanting to worship someone else in that way. I was, I kept telling myself, here to do those things that others want to do but don't do. I didn't want to simply watch things from the sidelines of my life.

Surprisingly, wherever I went in California, I couldn't get away from celebrity. When we pulled into the parking lot at the Marriot, we saw one of the most beautiful RV's that I had ever seen in my life. It was thirty feet of beautiful gray magnificence, polished and perfect. And in the rear it towed a jet black trailer out of which poured two lovely little scooters that, I could only assume, were used to run what a rich person might call—"little errands" around town. This was the RV of Laird Hamilton, surfer and workout guru extraordinaire. My teammates knew him right away. I had no clue who he was, but I have to admit that it was the first

89

time in my life that I had ever been that close to "someone" famous. I hate to admit it now, but he was undeniably impressive, an Adonis. And though people were impressed by his stature, they also expressed a bit of animosity towards his presence. To say that bicycle people are part of a tightly knit group is a bit of an understatement. Bike people form nothing short of a cult, a cult that does not want others intruding on its exclusive territory.

Hamilton's group was viewed with a bit of suspicion, as if a surfer was not only unwelcome at a bike race but also trampling on anointed, blessed, sacred and hallowed ground. Granted, this feeling was probably somewhat warranted and somewhat due to pure jealousy. Hamilton's RV was something to be reckoned with and taken very seriously. It was a thing of pure beauty, a luxury cruise liner to our hand-me-down Boston Whaler. Sure, they served the same purpose, but his looked great and would get his team there in style. In tow behind the RV was the small black pearl of a trailer. Even though we didn't admit it, the small Vespa style scooters inside were something we would've loved to possess.

He was also the evilest of all things to a bike team— the competition. To add insult to the already heinous injury of the whole discrepancy between the quality of our RVs,

Hamilton's trailer had a rack upon which his team had mounted around six surf boards. This was too much for my team to bear. It felt to us as if Hamilton were thumbing his nose in our general direction. This feeling was finally expressed in a series of incendiary commentary designed to make us feel better:

"How could anyone plan to bike across the country with a bunch of surfboards?"

"These guys are just a bunch of wheatgrass eating hippies!"

"Damn Hamilton. Damn him straight to Hell."

Of course this was useful for making us feel better. Of course, the rumors then began. There were rumors that began to make Laird Hamilton sound like he was a superhuman among superhumans:

"Didn't you hear? He paddled between all of the Hawaiian Islands on his surfboard, and he did it standing up!"

"I hear that he trained for this race by fitting a mountain bike with a metal sled. He's stacked iron plates on the back of the sled so he can tow it uphill! The guy's a monster."

I had to agree. He looked like a monster, not in the old-fashioned sense, but in the new "I'm bigger and stronger than anyone you will ever personally meet in your life sort of sense, so don't even bother trying to race against me."

These last speculations did nothing to inspire or

encourage the riders or the team to new and magically elevated levels of confidence, but they did provide some sick and demented fun. It was, after all, a race. All races need a level of good hearted ribbing and jesting about the other teams. As for finding out that Hamilton really was a larger than life monster of a man—it might have done the riders some good too. As least we had a small sense about what we were all up against.

Twenty

"If you can read this, then I'm ahead of you."—Mark Carney, crew member during the 2009 Race Across America, joking about a bumper sticker that he'd like to create for the race.

"I thought of that while riding a bike" Einstein speaking about his Special Theory of Relativity.

We stayed up that night thinking each and every one of us about the morning. In the morning, we raced, but none of us were ready for sleep. This was a mistake. We needed the sleep, but most of us stayed awake, thinking about the days to come. We were about to leave all the comfort of Oceanside and the posh Marriott behind, ready to begin our travelling caravan of fun and pain back towards the Atlantic, with its black waters lapping against Maryland's shore.

There are velocities and distances that we travel while on the land, in the water, or in the air—then there are the internal velocities and distances we travel in the mind. While the first are measured via movement through space and the revolutions of the hands on the clock that accompanies such movement, the second type of velocity and distance is quite different and much more difficult to measure. The mind is impelled by a journey or impels itself through some strange vortices where neither external movement nor momentum are

93

important, nor is the passage of time. I did not anticipate that my experience of time within the first few days of the RAAM would alter my general perception of the universe as much as it did, but it did. I don't claim to have any special or deep understanding of time. Of course, I'm in good company, because from what I've read, nobody seems to have any idea what time is.

For me, following a group of bicyclists across the country at the speed of a bicycle jolted my consciousness into a state of sublime recognition that time is, in fact, quite relative. It is relative mostly, in my very humble opinion, to the perception of various mental and physical stimuli in a person's surroundings. The feeling that time had somehow been altered began for me very early in the race. In fact, it seemed to start in the first few moments before the race's beginning. The race and all of the events of the race seemed somehow to escape the bonds of time for me. The intensity of the entire experience seemed to slow the movement of time.

Part of the reason for this strange sensation of timelessness may, I think, have had something to do with the sheer scale and magnitude of the race itself. It was an adventure with a scale unlike almost any other race on the planet. The course of the race itself, if it can even be considered a course, is divided into fifty-three so-called "time stations," which are spaced an average of fifty-seven miles apart from each other. Several of the time stations are over eighty-eight miles apart. These most distant time stations are located in either deserts—as in a particularly grueling section in California—or in Prairies—in Oklahoma and Kansas. The length of the 2009 race totaled three-thousand and twenty-one miles. This length varies from year to year, but always hovers around the back breakingly painful three-thousand mile mark. Another element that seemed to change the perception of time for me was the fact that much of the course forces teams to operate in remote areas of the continent. In quite a few sections, crews and racers must operate without the modern conveniences of GPS systems, cell phones, toilets, running water, medical facilities, or any other modernity.

A few of the time stations are manned by volunteer staff members, but many are unmanned, lending a further feeling of loneliness and isolation that I felt added to this bizarre feeling of timelessness. While the feeling gave me time for pause and contemplation, it also made me exhausted. I kept getting the eerie sensation that we had all been thrown into some anachronistic world where the absence of modern conveniences forced us into unlikely cooperation, interpersonal communication, and ultimately, a sense of community that is rarely, if ever, felt in the modern world.

Twenty-One

One of the deepest ironies of the RAAM is that while it may have felt to me as an escape from time, it is, of course, all about time. After all, it is a race.

The clock starts in Oceanside, California and stops only when the last racer crosses the finish line in Annapolis, Maryland. Each and every team has a simple mandate: call into RAAM headquarters within one half-hour of passing a time station. Failure to make the required call results in severe, although strangely delayed, penalties. These penalties take the form of a "time-out" of sorts that is spent waiting in a "penalty box" near the end of the race. Clearly this isn't even close to something that anyone would want to do after cycling nearly three-thousand miles.

To further complicate the team's perception and understanding of time during the race, all racers and their crew members must operate simultaneously in two distinct and separate conceptions of time. One of these is the local time that we are all used to. The other is known simply as "RAAM Time." RAAM Time operates on a twenty-four hour clock system, and it is set to the local Eastern Standard Time in Annapolis, Maryland, the ending point of the race. Local time is, of course, always local time. However, when RAAM teams pass a time station, they are each required to call in their times according to RAAM time. For instance, after reaching the first time station at Lake Henshaw, California—a devastatingly beautiful stretch of landscape located just 54.5 miles into the race—and climbing an impressive and nearly heartbreaking 2757 feet above sea level, all teams must call in their times. The fastest of these times might be called in as say, 19:21 on June 20th. This means that local time in California would be 7:21 P.M. This also means that the quickest and fastest team would've crossed the first time station just five hours and twenty-one minutes after the race started in Oceanside.

This may not sound all that impressive at first to some of us, even to competitive cyclists, but it must be taken into consideration that the preliminary 13.1 miles of the race are considered a "parade route". During the "parade route" portion, grandmothers, hippies, bikini-clad surfer girls, and small children are invited to ride along with the cyclists of the RAAM, all led by a police escort moving at a pleasant and relaxing pace. This initial parade route leads up through the winding roads so indicative of Southern California, up through the dry chaparral forest, up through the oceanic expansiveness of the orange groves, up through the timeless valleys, up through the undulations of the paved roads, and finally to the Old San Luis Rey River, which glitters along like a steel ribbon at the bottom of a steep ravine.

This is where the real fun begins. The racers, by this point having stripped away from the three-speed, pedal-pushing masses of RAAM wannabes, reconvene and regroup for what is called the "restart" of the race. This is the place where the race of truth really begins. The first portion is really just a joy ride, really. The Bonsall Bridge, spanning the river, is the reconvening point. Once the riders have reached the end of the "Parade Zone", the teams are re-assembled and restarted separately, with one-minute intervals between each competing team. The purpose of this, apparently, is to stagger each team sufficiently to prevent accidents and the overwhelming confusion that would result from a collective start. This is not, after all, a stage race, and riders do not compete in a peloton or mass of cyclists racing at breakneck speed towards a finish line.

From mile 12.8 through mile 21.3, the race continues in what the organizers have somewhat ominously dubbed the "unsupported race zone". This area of the course is something of an anomaly. It is an area where the racers must continue without the aid of support crews or support vehicles. Of course, this also means that racers must continue without the aid that these crew members and vehicles can provide. Any flat tires, injuries, mechanical failures, or any other such potential danger must be dealt with completely alone. Surely any misfortune during this portion of the race would be a devastating blow to both racer and team.

It is an odd beginning, in my opinion, because this type of "unsupported" zone is seen nowhere else in the entirety of the race. The opening of the race, with the carnival atmosphere in the first 12 miles and the "unsupported race zone" up to the 21st mile seem more like some sort of really bizarre test of a team's capacity to follow a multitude of directions as each flows along the winding and sinuous course.

During these 21 miles the race officials scrutinize every move that teams make, right down to the way a cyclists dismounts his bike to the way numbers are affixed to jerseys. Later in the race it seemed as though the officials were nearly non-existent. Of course, this wasn't actually the case. Some of the officials for the race, even at the start, are dressed in plain, civilian clothing. Others wear the official uniform of a RAAM official. No matter what they wear, they watch and scrutinize every move and every detail as if through the finely tuned lens of a microscope. I had the feeling that they were waiting and hoping for one of us to make a mistake. The whole thing was, for me at least, very disconcerting.

In addition to all this pressure, a rookie team—like

ours—is expected to perform as well as any of the other teams. None of the racers on our team had performed or competed in an event of this magnitude before. We were, in every sense of the term, "newbies".

Twenty-Two

At the end of the 21st mile, and beyond, racers continue with the assistance and help of their respective teams. There are still loads of restrictions. For example, between mile 21.3 and 54.5 there are "Allowed Support and Exchange Points". I can't even begin to remember how we kept track of it all, especially all those tenths of a mile.

The RAAM Routebook, AKA, the Race Bible, must be meticulously followed during all parts of the race from the beginning, and it provides all of this wonderful and confusing information. It provides maps, topographical elevations, turn by turn directions, mileage markers, and various and sundry tidbits about how far a team has gone and how far each team still has to go. This last bit of information is intimidating in the first half of the race and encouraging in the latter half. I think we all breathed a collective sigh of relief when the midpoint of the race was reached.

The Route Book graciously provides the locations of five designated "support and exchange points" between mile 21.3 and 54.5. Mile 54.5 marks the first of many Time Stations, where racers and teams must check in with their times. After the 54.5th mile, racers continue down the road in what the official rules call "Leapfrog Support", where the support vehicle, in our case a set of rented Toyota minivans, "leapfrogs" ahead of the cyclist on the road to a designated support point at which exchanges of water, food, etc., may be made. It is also at these specially designated points that teams are allowed to exchange racers, switching one cyclist off his bike so that another, presumably freshened and bright-eyed, cyclist may take over, with the idea of giving the relieved cyclist a much needed rest. Of course, this is only the theory. By the middle of the race, all plans are tossed in favor of what works at the moment. It's pretty much like everything else in life, "What works at the moment" becomes a mantra that is repeated through lips pressed together and then released as if saying a hushed prayer. God knows we were just hoping to make it through the first couple of miles unscathed.

Twenty-Three

The opening of the race is an act of deception on the part of the RAAM. The wrong impression is given of what the rest of the whole shebang is like. For much, hell, for most, of the opening of the race, the crew and the racers are separated from each other by the mysterious and invisible forces of the "rules" of the race, and this is certainly not even close to the case for the remainder.

The opening of the course, even with its difficulties, is staggeringly beautiful. The road winds its way through the parts of Southern California that are still rural and somewhat untarnished. The road rises and falls, weaves gently and in a quiet and gradual way through the chaparral forest. Manzanita trees, looking like awkward dragon limbs affected by rheumatoid arthritis, painfully twist into strange, contorted shaped, and in some places they writhe as snakes, trunks growing up then down, then up then down. They undulate across the parched earth, searching for water, bark flaked, worn, and ancient.

The well-maintained road dropped off menacingly in sections down deep embankments filled with cacti, and in other areas ascended into foothills and mountains, orange groves appearing here and there through the trees. The bright orange spheres of oranges dotted the leaves with a welcome splash of color. We passed by Harrah's Casino, a building more than just slightly out of place, as we took a turn in the road. Its festering wartiness sprouted from the landscape as a reminder of human activity in these otherwise unspoiled parts. We passed the sprawling complex not because we didn't want to stop but because we were following a small figure ahead of us on a bike as he pumped his legs to an internal metronome.

The other members of our team, following behind us in another van, stopped. They pulled one-arm bandits, puttered around the dank interior of the building, all the while pushing the limits of another human endeavor that seems in some sense closely aligned with this race: gambling. It got me to thinking about how this race really was a big gamble. I suppose every race is.

Every racer prepares and trains for extended periods of time, hoping and praying that his legs, heart, and mind are steadfast enough to win. But like almost everything else in life, all this preparation—up to a full year or more of it, sometimes a lifetime of pedal pushing, yoga, dietary restrictions, etc.—is wagered against the possibility of winning. Robert Burns in translation: "The best laid plans of mice and men go oft awry." The stakes are high, both monetarily, for an extremely large amount of money is spent of the race, and also physically and mentally. Each racer faces distinct and unpleasant possibilities. Anything can happen out here: crashes, accidents with cars, flat tires, theft of bicycles, dehydration, exhaustion, muscle problems, saddle sores, lightning strikes, even the potential for what some might consider the ultimate catastrophe, death.

As we rode past Harrah's, we tried not to think about that possibility. We followed the bicycle in front of us to Lake Henshaw, the first checkpoint on the race. We stopped in the dust and brittle air in a town that looked more like a train wreck than anything else.

Dust was everywhere, covering the trailers, covering the road, getting into everything. We stopped the van and let the engine tick away while the other support vehicle, with their racers—Tim Bryant and Chaney Becker—raced on ahead. Lake Henshaw itself, laying in a pocket that appears to be pushed by the fist of a giant into the earth, is opposite of a trading post type store and restaurant of the sort that only appears in isolated areas, the kind of place that serves breakfasts and dinner at the same time and where no one gives a second glance to anyone or anything. The lake itself is really something incredible to look at, a beautiful jewel in the barren desert. I wondered how such a vast amount of water got there. It was late June. The grasses around the lake were dry and brittle, bleached by the sun to bone brightness. I had to squint to focus the light into any sort of bearable brightness. There was palpability to the air and the colors of that place. Everything was crisp, distinct. The heat too was crisp and dry, as if all the available moisture had been pulled from the atmosphere. The lake, I supposed, had taken it all. It was the only place with water.

I wandered around the parking lot of the "Lake Henshaw Café", watching the racers and crews from other teams. They were sprawled everywhere. There was a little shade provided by a few trees that someone had planted in raised beds in the parking lot. It was here that I finally noticed Chris Lake, bent in two like a paperclip. He was busy emptying the contents of his stomach at the base of a tree.

He had just finished pushing an incredible fifty-four miles and was completely overheated. His vomit pooled in tiny pockets of the soil. In the shade Chris's body trembled and his hands shivered. His mistake was overexertion in this first portion of the race—a mistake that could have been deadly. Overexertion can lead to dehydration, and there was no doubt that Chris was suffering from a lack of water. The acrid smell of vomit was in the air. Chris has become, in the parlance of the other members of the team, "toast", that is to say, "finished, kaput, done."

At the Lake Henshaw checkpoint we still had 2,962.9 miles left to go, and things weren't looking too good from what I could tell. Clearly, the beginning of the race was not going well. The total elevation that Chris and Jim had climbed at this point was 2,767.0 feet, and 2000 feet of this climb was done from around mile 40 to mile 45. That's 2000 vertical feet of climbing in less than five miles, no joke here. Much of this climbing had been done by Jim.

Chris had actually had a few issues before arriving at Lake Henshaw, puking a few times on the way. Jim had taken over, wracking his own body in an attempt to give Chris time to rest. This ended up being one of the biggest mistakes of the entire race. Once both had spent their energy the first day it seemed nearly impossible to recuperate fully for the remainder. At the time it seemed to be a nearly insurmountable task, akin to saying that a mountain climber planning to ascend Everest had run out of stream in the scree field but still planned to reach the summit.

Twenty-Four

The team began to come undone, to slowly unravel. Instead of moving forward we came to a painful and grinding halt. While Tim and Chaney took over, followed by the black chase van and its crew, we made our way to a brief rest stop. The RV followed in lukewarm pursuit. A Wal-Mart parking lot seemed the most appealing place to rest our tires for a while, so we pulled in. The Wal-Mart company regularly allows RV campers to use their parking lots as rest areas and camping spots.

Yes, they even allow sleeping overnight. Who knows how long this arrangement will last? It seems like a disaster waiting to happen, if you ask me. These oases in the land of highways and backroads became places where we stopped as we made our way across the good ol' U. S. of A. Usually we had the company of a least a couple of other teams competing in the RAAM. We rarely made any contact with them, preferring sleep over socialization. Damn shame really. But what were we to do? We were dead tired. We pulled in and parked the white minivan, which by this point had been affectionately dubbed "white-heat". It could just as easily been named "big-stink" or "hell on wheels". I suppose "white-heat" had a better ring to it at the time. Jim LaBelle trundled over to the RV, limping along. He collapsed on the thinly padded bench seat across from the Formica topped folding dining table. I'll tell you, one look at his face was enough to see that he was in more pain than most could imagine. The weird part of it was that he wasn't making much of an expression at all. There was in place of a grimace a vague veiled look to his eyes that made it look like he was seeing something that no one else could. Whatever it was was hovering in front of him.

Existential crisis or pain or both—it didn't look good. He laid on his right side, head propped on one arm, pillow dashed between his legs to relieve pressure, his Blackberry phone (the "crackberry") held in left hand, which lay upon the gray fabric of the bench. His gaze shifted, at first imperceptibly, then noticeably, to the front screen of the device, where he had chosen a photo of his two children as wallpaper. His focus became slightly more relaxed as he stared at them with their faces gently smiling back at him. I thought immediately about what Jim had said to me when I first met him in his bike shop: "I want to prove to my children that anything is possible." That's what he had been saying to himself over and over again. The idea that anything is possible was one of the main reasons Jim had wanted to compete in the race, but now his back was destroyed. His back had been bothering him for days before the race, a severe penalty for years of bike racing, a penalty of living for a dream.

Meanwhile, outside the minivan Chris Lake looked like a china doll, porcelain white skin and bright red lips filled with arterial blood. Sweat had gathered in cool little beads along his forehead, and was trickling down his face in rivulets that appeared to have a divine right to descend towards the dry and parched pavement, where the sun baked them white and salty. I asked him if he was okay and if he needed anything. Of course, in hindsight this was a ludicrous thing to ask. The obvious truth was that he was not okay, but it didn't appear like he'd readily admit it.

Neither Jim nor Chris had come over three-thousand miles, trained for a race like this, and given up so much just to admit defeat. It started to become clear that they wouldn't quit, not yet. Chris had a primal look come into his eyes, one that said, "I need rest and I need water, but I will not be defeated." The water bottle in his right hand trembled, condensation on the exterior dripping to the same point on the pavement where his sweat and tears has crusted over just moments before. He rose on his legs as if suspended by wires and made his way to the RV. About ten feet into his walk he bent over like a marionette and vomited between his feet. The watery bile spread across the ground, seeping into the pavement, spreading like a drop of blood on finely woven cloth. He regained balance and focus and walked again, determinedly, towards the RV. This time he made it to the steps, sat partially in the shade. For a brief moment he looked startlingly like Rodin's Thinker statue brought to life, sweat saturating his hair. The doorway of the RV looked like a cavernous mouth gaping behind him, swallowing the white light of the sun, framing Chris in a rectangle of darkness that made him suddenly appear like a religious icon in a niche in a cathedral. His bowed head added to the illusion, giving the appearance of a crucified man.

I crept by him, squeezing through to the RV's interior, into that darkness, escaping the eyes of passersby, escaping the heat of the light, to see the others within. It took several moments for my eyes to adjust to the light. When they did, everything was cast with a film yellow haze. The interior of the RV went from jet black to crimson to scarlet and finally began to take on the colors of life. When I wiped the sweat from my eyes I cast a glance towards Jim. He was still immobilized from his Herculean effort on the mountain. From talking with the crew I knew that many of us felt his actions were deliriously irresponsible. Some felt that he should've held back, that he should've stuck to his original plan. The plan had been simple and straightforward.

Each rider was supposed to have taken to the road for ½ hour at a time, and then have switched off with someone else. This was what the plan had been for as far back as any of us could remember. It was what we had discussed at all of the team meetings and it was LaBelle's idea.

He had broken his own rules.

Jim Bernard crouched in the front of the RV with a look of extreme concern on his face. Hesselbarth, the photographer, peered wide eyed through his Graphlex large format camera. His Nikon swung freely from his neck. It was clear he had no intention of taking a photograph in this moment.

We heard soft whimpering from the steps of the RV. Jim Bernard rose to his feet and made his way over to Chris, who had begun weeping softly. It was a gray sort of whimper. Soft as rain and hard as calloused snow. It was a compressed expression of everything that had gone wrong. It was a sound that made many of us doubt whether we could go on. We averted our eyes. Bernard spoke to him in a gentle voice, full of compassion. "Everyone knows what you feel, man. We've all been there. We've all been you." Chris sat in the door and took a long and deep breath. This is the reality of the race. People can get sick, hurt, and sometimes they have to stop. That's all there is to it. "There's not a single person here that would hold it against you," said

Bernard. Of course, this is not true. Someone would almost certainly resent it. But Chris was not the type to give up. Not by a long shot. Jim continued in a whisper, "You've busted your ass for eight months and everyone knows that." Silence. "Come on, we're going to Cottonwood to find you a real medic or a hospital and the worst case scenario is that you will have to finish with the crew and the team will continue as a three person team. Come on. You're coming with us in the van."

Bernard is a good man.

Some of the crew thought that Chris had a virus. Jim LaBelle was among this camp, and he asked us to sanitize the RV a bit. I grabbed a roll of paper towels, happy to have something else to do besides my awkward staring and scratching of notes in my little black book. I fumbled with the roll a wee bit, pulling off long streamers that looked disturbingly like flags of surrender. The wind came rushing through the door and the banner of defeat waved in the hot breeze, fanning our general discontent into a simmering worrying anger. I grabbed a container of hand sanitizer and went to work. A thick chemical enthusiasm filled the air. Jim LaBelle seemed to perk up at the smell. He looked over at me and finally spoke. "Ok. So here's the deal. We're going to a hotel in Cottonwood to regroup and to decide what we want to do next. We've gotta see if we really want to do this. I don't feel like I'm giving up, but I'd like to be a wise human being." There was no longer a look of defeat in his eyes but a look of resolve that everyone on the team came to expect from him—the resolve to continue.

This is the resolve that passes down through generations of humanity. It is the resolve that comes to people at the edge of giving up. It is the resolve that comes when we are brought to the edge of what we think is possible. Then, we push closer, closer, and closer, until finally we are right on the fringe of this world, and then, suddenly, we are back on the strong footing of the earth below our feet once more, moving along again.

This approach to life takes fearlessness. It takes the knowledge that humanity has a tremendous capacity to achieve but that in order to achieve we must take enormous risks. We must be willing to push ourselves into areas in which we feel more than discomfort, in which we may face the final outcome. We must move right to the edge of the darkness.

This is where Jim wanted to go. It's where all of us on the crew wanted to go. We wanted to see what we were made of, to test our grit in this world. It is why we could not and would not give up.

After this brief statement from Jim, everyone felt a rush of new energy. Jim Bernard and I got Chris to crash out on a makeshift bed in the back of one of the vans. Then, we talked. Jim Bernard was yet convinced that we should continue. As crew chief, Bernard had a difficult role to play. Making decision for racers who had reached their limits was not fun or easy, but it was why he was there. He felt the race was over. According to Bernard, Labelle and Chris were "toast". He felt that we should all go home—curtains for the dream—safety first. Of course, he was in many ways right. After all, people have died on races like this.

Bike racing is and probably always will be a particularly cruel sport. Being a crew chief during a race is no joke. Jim's position was a difficult one. People's lives are in his hands. Ultimately he decided that we should stop the race. Of course, like any team, there are a lot of people involved, and the real decision never sits on only one person's shoulders.

The information about quitting the race was relayed to Chaney and Tim, who'd chosen to continue racing, to forge on ahead as planned in the slim hope that Jim and Chris would make a full recovery in six-hours, when it would be time to switch shifts.

When they heard that the race might potentially be

done and over, they were defiant. Tim said it best. "We came here to race, and we're going to fucking race. I didn't come here to fucking quit; I came to fucking win the Race Across America." Chaney, in his quiet way, agreed by saying, "Yeah, we should keep going." They would continue. This was incredible, for they had no idea how much longer they would be racing for, nor did they know what toll the length of time they would be on the road might take on their bodies. They just wanted to ride.

Twenty-Five

Next stop: Hospital. Jim heard from the doctors what he already knew. His back was fucked. It was 4:21 on June 2nd. We've all had about two hours of sleep since the race began. Two hotel rooms became our crash pads in Cottonwood. Hot showers and low morale.

Distance covered: 437.6 miles.

Distance left: 2,579.8 miles.

No one knew if we could make it. This journey had just begun but its end was no longer clear. At the hospital, Chris was being given an IV drip with saline. He seemed to be perking up. This was the last time I would see Jim and Chris for any length of time. After the incident, Bernard transferred me from White Heat to the black minivan nicknamed Big Business, which served as Chaney and Tim's support vehicle. It was here that the journey began to take on a bit more of the color of an epic struggle. And it was at this point that I began the descent into my mind where a chaos began to take root that can only be described as bordering on insanity.

Twenty-Six

Mortality is a funny thing when you think about it too long. It's one thing to contemplate life and death at home or on a beach a ten minute drive from civilization. It's a different thing altogether when riding through the emptiness of an Arizona desert and the temperature is 110 degrees and cell phone coverage is non-existent and the water supply is limited and the vehicle is running low on fuel. That's something entirely different.

Twenty-Seven

I rode in Big Business, the minivan, for the rest of the trip. It was cleaner that White Heat and had a sense of order to it that the other van did not. We drove out of Cottonwood onto SR 89A, passing an old grocery store with the obvious and uncreative name "Food City". We headed out of town crossing the unpretentious Verde River, which does not indeed live up to its name, instead running perfectly clear, and we soon entered Coconino National Forest. Jim and Chris were resting in the RV. It was unclear just how long it would take them to recover or if they would at all during the race.

Twenty-Eight

Once we were in the Coconino National Forest the road began to climb fairly steadily, becoming quite steep at points, finally topping out at 7007.4 feet. We headed towards Flagstaff. The night began to fall across the desert sky, turning the heavens red. I switched from Big Business to the RV, which had recently been dubbed the "Ranchero Bernardo" after Jim Bernardo. We headed towards Tuba City, following the cyclists and Big Business. Tuba City is in the middle of the Navajo Nation. There's hardly anything to it, really, but we looked forward to seeing a spot of civilization anyway.

Twenty miles into the ride we received a cell phone call from the others in the team asking us to pick up something to eat, so we turned around and headed the twenty miles back to Flagstaff. This, frankly, seemed to piss everyone off, but the drive to obtain food seemed to outweigh the drive to move forward in the race, and I thought, "What the hell, what's another forty miles?" Finally, after many turns and much finagling, we found an Italian place. It was one of those places that would make you feel right at home the second you walked in, full of old furnishings and dark colors. It was filled with the smell of garlic and baking bread. My heart fluttered at the thought of all that food. Mark Carney, John Hesselbarth and I walked in in all our splendor and grubby glory and ordered ten delicious meals to go. In hindsight, I'm surprised that they allowed us in at all, as we looked like we were under the influence of a combination of crack and sleeping pills, which might as well have been the case, especially considering the level of absolute sleep-deprived imbecility we had reached. We told the waiter, whose face had turned into a gaping hole of a mouth, that we had but twenty minutes to get all the meals and get the hell out of there. After he had managed to thinly conceal his disgust, he discussed the race with us. He was one of those people who I found it difficult to talk with, the type who smiled and nodded as if he understood but who I would like to give a good crack across the mouth for being so "goddamn phony", as our friend Holden Caulfield might have said.

Frankly, I couldn't tell if he was actually interested or if he thought we were lying about the whole thing. He smiled and listened, nodding all the while, but it was in the way the people generally do when they think that you are a bit mad or insane or crazy. We tried to explain a bit about the race, mumbled a few apologies about why we looked the way we did. We were smelly and stinking and looked like a sad bunch. The way the restaurant staff looked at us, combined with the sleep deprivation, made me feel like perhaps I was crazy. The thought of my possible insanity entered my mind and clung there for a while. I couldn't decide what to say next, and I was starting to contemplate lunging at this man for being so "goddamn phony" and ripping his "goddamn head off", so I excused myself and crept over to a couch the restaurant had set up and set myself down in heap. It was one of those beautiful antique Victorian couches. It had a high curvaceous back and material that felt like warm butter, a velvet softness that spread over my legs and hands and the back of my neck like the black of night, covering my spirit and soul. I soon gave way to an overwhelming wave of sleep.

It was useless to fight against it by this point. My brain, after so many hours of sleep deprivation, was on the brink of total and complete meltdown. Then, without warning, I was asleep. It was the sort of sleep that I can only liken to having an anvil dropped on my head. I fell forward and somersaulted into the blackness in the back of my mind. It was as if something inside my head had become detached and was flapping around behind my eyelids. I felt myself falling backward, then jerked out of the sleeping fit just as quickly as I had fallen in. The waiter was staring at me, but he quickly averted his eyes. People don't like to let lunatics know that they're being watched. It soon felt to me like they wanted us to leave. It may have been because they were pushing us out of the door. John Hesselbarth snapped a few photos and we were on our way, Styrofoam bundles of steaming Italian delights carried in our arms.

Twenty-Nine

We headed from Flagstaff towards Tuba City, deep in the Navajo Nation. We had been warned about the place. At about thirty-nine miles from Flagstaff the racecourse enters the Navajo Nation and the clocks shift from Mountain Standard to Mountain Daylight Time. I thought that it felt a lot more like we had shifted to Navajo Time. There was something mystical about saying that to myself. "Navajo Time!" As if I had entered some new realm. I liked the phrase so much that I kept repeating to myself: "Navajo Time! Navajo Time! Navajo Time!" My mind was getting weirder and weirder. We became the guests of the tribes from that point on, all the way to Pagosa Springs, over three hundred miles away.

We had been warned about being on our best behavior and about being weary of the place. Veteran racers had told us before we had left California that this could be a dangerous strip of land to travel, that the tribal cultures that lived here were not always friendly, and that we should not, under any circumstances, stop to chat, especially at night. There were a few stories circulating about racers who had been left alone during the daylight hours who had been jumped, their bikes stolen, their bodies beaten. They had been left in 100 degree heat in the middle of the desert, left only with the hope that their support vehicle would come sooner rather than later to relieve them of their misery. We passed through at night, so the heat was not a problem, but in the back of my mind, I kept thinking about being jumped, beaten, and left for dead.

The night was now fully upon us and it was so dark that it was almost impossible to see beyond the hundred foot throw of the headlights. There was no moon, only the stars, weakly illuminating the desert land. As we moved the darkness, despite these stories of horror and assault and mayhem, became a comforting sort of visual noise. We couldn't see a thing, so I felt safe. In the day, I had heard, this land is breathtakingly beautiful. The roadside growth quickly drops off and the sedimentary layers of the cliffs in the areas are supposed to be striped with gray, red, white, yellow and brown.

Before I had been there, I imagined that the desert would be a place devoid of life. But now, even in the darkness, I had been able to make out the shapes of various plants illuminated by our headlights on the side of the road, and I could imagine the animals that lived there. Each and every square inched seemed to contain some form of life. The animosity of the indigenous culture seemed light years away.

It was somewhere in Navajo Country that things began to go worse for me mentally. I had called my wife with reasonable regularity up until that point, but from what she's told me, I didn't make a shred of sense even after one day without sleep. Trying to find the narrative strand in sleep deprived darkness is close to impossible.

Thirty

I hope that you, dear reader, will forgive this additional interruption of the narrative for a moment. The change in the structure of the text from this point on demands at least some mention. The nearly complete abandonment of a linear progression to things, from this point onward in the text will, I hope, be forgiven. If the narrative jumps from one subject to the next, or if it meanders even more than it has already between disparate temporal locals, it is because from this point on in the race my mind was so destroyed by a lack of sleep that keeping a strict narrative became almost impossible. I had, quite literally, lost my mind. I was, on occasion, hallucinating, even more incoherent than usual, and, as my wife could attest from my sporadic phone calls, on the brink of insanity by almost any definition of the word.

Thirty-One

Mexican Hat, Utah is named for a peculiar rock formation in the Oljato-Monument Valley. According to most accounts, the name "Mexican Hat" derives from the strange shape of a sixty foot wide, twelve foot thick outcropping of rock that appears to teeter precariously on a thin pedestal located near the northeast edge of the town. Rock climbers from around the world come to climb the two routes that ascend to the "summit".

The rock, from a distance at least, looks curiously like a sombrero. Upon closer inspection it looked to me more like a cow patty cast into rock. So, rock climbers travel from all over the world to climb a piece of shit. We cycled and drove, cycled and drove. In spite of—or perhaps because of—the lack of sleep, things began to feel pretty normal again. I started to have the odd feeling that chasing after a cyclist in a small minivan was what I had always done and what, perhaps, I would always do. We'd follow Chaney for a bit, say an hour or so, then give him the signal that it was time to switch off with Tim. We'd drive ahead of Chaney, get Tim saddled up on his carbon-fiber horse, then as Chaney "crossed-wheels" with Tim to meet the demands of race protocol, Tim would take off. This was how it went all across Utah, and this is how it'd go all across the country.

Passing through Monument Valley is passing through a dreamscape. The land, composed mostly of rocks, had not a single ounce of weight to it as we passed through. Things danced and hovered in front of my vision like lonely ghosts. The sun was rising when we began our passing through, which made the journey through the valley all the more surreal. The rocks seemed to come alive as the orange light suffused the atmosphere, distilling the world into cosmic luminescence.

Shadows faded and fell, stars reeled away, and we were for the first time on the trip drunk on the expanse of the world, the horizon rippling with the heat of the coming day. I felt my soul in my throat, my body ethereal and pure. I could see why this was a place of the gods. The proportions are amazing. The geography of the place is stunning. The Navajo call this place Tse Bii Ndzisgaii, meaning the "valley of the rocks". Towering sandstone buttes stagger across the floor of the valley, great hulking beasts of stone. It wasn't hard to imagine the powerful forces that carved this place. I felt like I was in the dried bed of an ancient and enormous river or amid the leftover shambles of a beautiful apocalypse.

About twenty-five miles from Mexican Hat, after passing through the Valley of the Gods and by the San Juan River, we stopped in Bluff, Utah by the side of the road.

Ellen McNally, the team's chiropractor, pulled a mat out and placed it on the sandy soil about twenty feet from the minivan and gave Chaney a quick massage and an adjustment while Tim rode on. About a mile down the road we stopped again at the Twin Rocks Trading Post, located beneath the "Navajo Twins" geologic formation. Owners and native sons Barry and Steve Simpson claimed to have established the trading post at the "Intersection of Tradition and Innovation". A location, I assumed, which also provided a steady and reliable cash-flow in this harsh and seemingly unforgiving environment. The trading post was filled with contemporary American Indian art, books, trinkets, knick-knacks, and local newspapers—including the Navajo Times—and a restaurant. It was the latter that we were mostly interested in.

We ordered some Navajo Omelets, which ended up being served to go in convenient Styrofoam containers that latched shut with a sort of tongue and groove type set up. The omelets were enormous. True monstrosities as far as breakfast food went. The entire egg, bacon, and cheese mixture was wrapped up in what they call Navajo "fry bread," which believe me is as deadly as it is delicious. We ate every last scrap as we drove through some of the most divine landscape on earth, more interested in filling our bellies than gazing out at the red rocks. Billions of years of weather and time showing off for us and all we could do was follow a bicycle and think of cramming calories. Go figure.

The "Navajo Twins" rock formation stands right behind the "Navajo Twins" Trading Post, a rock formation whose grandeur is a fitting testament to the landscape and the people who still inhabit it. Interestingly, the Navajo, as we call them, were originally given the name Ni'hooka Diyan Dine-sometimes shortened to Dine—by their creators. The full name means "Holy Earth People," though now shortened by most to "Dine," means "The People". My guess is that "Ni'hooka Diyan Dine" never really caught on. It was the Tewa people who called themselves "Navahu", meaning "large area of farmland" or "large area of cultivated land". But most accounts the name was changed to "Navaho" around 1630 in a book by Alonso de Benavides, who was a Portuguese Franciscan missionary in the New Mexico area way back in the early 1600s.

As the Navajo creation story goes, the Holy People emerged from the three underworlds into this world, called the "glittering world", through a magical reed. At this point they built a sweat lodge, met up in the first house—a Hogan—and set about the important work of setting up the world in an orderly fashion, which included placing mountains in their proper locations and identifying four sacred stones that would mark the boundaries of their homeland. After this was done, presumably they were tired out, but they continued by having a lengthy discussion about placing the stars in their proper places. Alas, the Coyote man, known as a devilish trickster, got tired of waiting around because of the long discussion about what should go where, so he decided to take care of the business by himself, grabbing the edge of a blanket upon which rested the stars and flinging the remaining stars into the sky, where they still reside today. This explains their pleasing randomness, I suppose.

The Holy People continued to make all the other features of the Earth, like clouds, trees, rain, and so forth. They put the moon and the sun into the sky. Then, evil monsters began to appear and began to kill the new Earth people. Luckily, Ever-Changing woman, Asdzaa Nadleehe, married the sun and bore two sons, twins who became the heroes of the Navajo people. They were known as "Child-Born-of-Water" and "Monster Slayer". The twins made an arduous journey to their father, the sun, who gave them lightning bolts to fight the monsters. Every place that the twins killed a monster, the monster turned to stone. The giant, nearly monolithic, rock formations in the landscape are seen as the bodies of these monsters turned to stone. The twin rocks, enormous pillars of stone, represent the two twins whose power saved the world.

Thirty-Two

By about 1:40 PM Mountain Time, we were well on our way out of Utah and the land of the Navajo and headed into the heart of the Colorado Rockies. It was 3:40 PM RAAM Time, something we hadn't completely lost track of, because by necessity we needed to report all of our time station stops in that particular format. We were headed for Durango, Colorado. (Yee Haw! Durangoooooooooo!) We had been on the road, non-stop, since Flagstaff, and Chaney and Tim were ready for a much needed rest, to say the least. We continued up into higher elevations, watching the desert turn to forest, the red rocks to bluish-gray. The course continues on US 160 E, gradually climbing to a maximum elevation of 8, 417.7 feet. We pulled off the side of the road to crash somewhere around 8,000 feet. The crew with Jim LaBelle and Chris Lake trucked on ahead while we set up a quick stop for rest. The RV pulled in behind us and a few people crept in, crashing out on hastily unrolled sleeping pads and bags, while the bed in the back became the exclusive domain of the two weary cyclists. We ate more food, of course. Some sort of pasta mixture, composed of what, I can't remember.

A few of us crept outside and crawled into sleeping bags and bivy sacks under the glare of headlamps and also of headlights passing. This high altitude was the dominion of the trees, conifers that were silhouetted against a strangled and dark sky. We slept like the dead for two hours then woke and jumped back in the vans, ready again to leapfrog with the other half of our team, people with whom by this point we had almost no contact. In the two hours I slept I managed to get bitten by a tick behind my right knee. When I returned home from the race I would have to go through a series of tests at Tufts Medical Center in Boston to determine if I had been a victim of Rocky Mountain Fever, a tick-borne disease that is considered one of the deadliest bacterial infections in the United States. The tests finally concluded that I did not, in fact, have the "tick typhus" as it is sometimes called but a particularly bizarre presentation of Lyme disease. Life has so many wonderful little ironies.

From that stop in the mountains it was downhill all the way to Durango, Colorado. The RV and sleeping riders headed for the Santa Rita Park Visitor's Center while a few of us went into town to buy overpriced food at the local co-op. By the time we got back with the shopping, everyone was passed out inside the RV, except for Ed Zabilski, who seemed to me to hover just on the edge of bodhisattva consciousness, and Jim Bernard, who hovered on his cell phone. The visitor's center is right on the Animas River, an ice cold torrent of glacial melt off that pounds down its course like a freight train. I walked down to the water's edge and plunged into the icy water. The river nearly swallowed me whole, and I felt the weight of my entire being pulling me deeper into the water. My muscles contracted, and every fiber of my being jolted back into itself, until finally, I emerged from the water reborn. I remembered thinking at the beginning of the trip that we'd have tons of time to go sightseeing and see the country, but this was the first time we had stopped long enough for more than a piss and snooze on the side of the road. It felt as if I were revived from the dead, at least for a few minutes.

From the Animas River we followed the road to beautiful Pagosa Springs, stopping in the middle of town to wait for the riders. In the center of the town is a beautiful hot spring that smells, unfortunately, of sulfur. We stopped briefly to regroup again, and several of us splashed the stinking water from the spring on our faces. It seemed like a good idea at the time. I started laughing out loud about something that Chaney had said. Upon returning to the van, he had said, "I think my muscles are conspiring against me. One gets jealous over what the other one is doing and starts to revolt!" Clearly, I wasn't the only one losing his mind. This was a great consolation to me. Really, it was.

Thirty-Three

We blasted through Pagosa Springs, the whole half-witted lot of us, and headed towards Chama, New Mexico. The road, US 160 East, was one of the most scenic I had ever been on, descending through large swaths of woodland in the San Juan National Forest. In this section of the race we passed in and out of New Mexico as the road meanders back and forth across the border between New Mexico and Colorado. With what little mental ability I had left, I looked down into the RAAM guidebook (a.k.a. the RAAM Bible), and sighed in dismay. In sharp contrast to the section we had just completed, which was difficult but full of short climbs, in the upcoming section there were one or two long climbs.

The first section, according to the book, paralleled, "the narrow gauge Cumbres and Toltec Scenic Railroad". Perhaps on my next trip across the country, I thought. But certainly not now. The second long climb would take us over the highest point in the RAAM, La Manga Pass. The Pass is, according to the guidebook, 10, 250 feet above sea level, though a topographical map I consulted years later told me it was 10, 230 feet above sea level. Any way you cut it, it's both an accomplishment and a slice of hurt me pie for the poor cyclist asked to push his bulk up the slope. In this case, the honor of the climb fell to Tim Bryant, the specialist of long, flat stretches. The world is full of cruel little ironies.

The descent of approximately 4,000 feet from La Manga Pass into Taos, New Mexico was a reprieve from the brutal ascents. We stopped the RV for a while, Chris Lake and Jim LaBelle took their turns at this point while Tim Bryant and Chaney took a rest in the minivan. At the time I think that they were so tired that they would've slept anywhere. I remember vaguely wondering why they weren't sleeping in the RV, since it was available. The air was cold, maybe 40-50 degrees Fahrenheit. Just a day ago we were topping 110 degrees in the desert. It was June 23rd, around 4:38 RAAM time (2:38 A.M. local time), though to be completely honest, I didn't give a damn about what day it was, and I scarcely could have told you if it was 2:38 A.M. or P.M. if you had asked me.

I slunk into the RV and mixed myself a cup of what I can honestly say is the worst instant coffee I had ever had in my entire existence. Actually, I can probably safely say that it will likely be the worst cup of coffee I will ever have. I have here included the recipe, should you ever desire to attempt killing yourself:

Sutcliffe's Justly Famous Wake-Up Juice

1 Cup Tepid RV Water, possibly polluted with bacterial growth

5 Heaping Dirty Tablespoons of expensive Trader Joe's Instant Coffee

1 Cup of Raspberry OWater (for the sake of supporting your sponsor)

Take all ingredients and stir weakly

Make sure that instant coffee granules

DO NOT DISSOLVE

Choke down entire concoction using spoon to cram down throat, if necessary.

Repeat as often as needed until rigor mortis has set in. I plunked myself down on the RV's couch for what may have been ten minutes or an hour, and opened my eyes when I felt everything moving under me. Jim Bernard, was driving, eyes fixed intently on the road. I stood up and made my way somewhat uneasily towards the front passenger seat, tripping over clothes that had slipped from the seats to the floor. Jim smiled at me as I sat down, and said something to the effect of, "I see you're still in the land of the living. So, is it everything you'd imagined?" I replied that it was, "all that and more." We spoke then about Jim LaBelle and Chris Lake, who were at that very moment moving towards Taos.

At least one of them would be on a bike. We were looking forward to the next checkpoint. In fact, most of the time we were looking forward to the checkpoints. Each one made us feel as if we were getting somewhere. Chaney, who had stayed in the minivan with Tim, called my phone at that moment. His main concerns: 1. "The condition of the RV is deplorable." 2. "What will Jim and Chris have for breakfast?" Increasingly as the trip progressed, all of the cyclists became more and more concerned, preoccupied really, with food. I can't say I blame them. They were going through calories like they were going out of style, and I think it became more of an instinctive response to worry about food more than anything else. I told Jim Bernard what Chaney had said and he simply replied, "The crazier things become, the more we need to focus. There's a real danger of not focusing. People came out here to get as close as possible to the abyss, feel it, smell it, and then go home. But we've gotta make sure that they actually get home. I'm worried about these guys." The thing was, out there, it was the blind leading the blind. We were headed, as far as I could tell, into the gaping maw of hell. The devils were going to welcome us with open arms and piles of cow patty sandwiches.

On the way into Taos, we followed "Earthship Way",

which has to be seen to be truly appreciated. I have to admit, even before going on the Race Across America, I had been a fan of Earthships. I say this only because I think it's fair you know who you're dealing with, and my description of what an "Earthship" is will likely focus on the rosy, fun, and coolness factors rather than any of the potential downfalls of living in a house made out of earth filled tires. That's right folks, Earthships are houses constructed of old rubber tires that have been laid down flat in tiers, like bricks, and as they are laid down, each tire is filled with dirt.

The dirt is then pounded using either a sledgehammer or a gas-powered thing-a-ma-do, causing the entire tire and earth combination to attain the structural integrity of say, a rock. Most Earthships have been dug into the ground to develop an "earthy" thermal mass, which helps them to maintain a comfy year round temperature of around 55-60 degrees, and this is without supplemental heating or cooling. The exterior of an Earthship looks like a cross between a mound of soil and a spaceship. Most Earthships are designed to take full advantage of solar gain from the sun, and many have banks of solar panels for electricity, gray water recycling systems, attached greenhouses or growing spaces, and other hippie inspired do-dads that their builders claim will change the world. I tend to favor these ideas, and though

I haven't been inside an Earthship personally, I think I'd like to have one. The people who build them seem to have a fierce independence and penchant for living on the edge of the world, and believe me, the edge of Taos is at least close to the edge of the world. Upon reflection, Earthships are perfect in a place like Taos. You see, an Earthship would be just as much at home on another planet as it would in Taos, and Taos is unlike any place I've ever been. It is, essentially, its own special little planet.

We pulled into Taos, approaching on US 64E towards the Rio Grande Gorge Bridge, which has got to be one of the most beautiful and striking steel arch bridges in the world. Quite frankly, I haven't got a clue about how many other steel arch bridges are out there, but this one was beautiful, and that's not a description that I usually would use to describe a bridge. The bridge itself spans 1, 280 feet across the Rio Grande River (go figure), and hovers an impressive 565 feet above the water at the bottom of the gorge. A wrong turn off this bridge would most certainly not end happily (read: crash and burn and die a miserable death).

We stopped in Taos, albeit briefly, for what had become our favorite way of passing the time: finding food. The location for our culinary adventure this time was the Best Western Kachina Lodge, which also happened to be the finish line for the RAAM's sister race, The Race Across the West. The "RAW", as it has been dubbed, follows essentially the same route as the RAAM, starting in Oceanside, California, but finds its termination here, at the noble and imposing facade of the Best Western. It too is a very, very difficult race.

The Best Western must have been, how shall I say this, designed by someone emboldened by a sense of South Western flair that I had never before encountered and will likely never encounter again. We wandered in, my fellow explorers and I, into the hearty interior of the Kachina Lodge expecting, I don't know, a few tables and some food. But boy oh boy, instead we were in for a treat. The interior of the dining area, a lofty place to be sure, resembled a yurt in design. The cylindrical dining room was surmounted by a conical roof with enormous timbers, and the whole of the roof structure was supported by a gargantuan totem pole which appeared to be crafted out of rebar reinforced concrete, which was then painted in a gaudy fashion. This mammoth phallus gazed down upon us with its many beady eyes as we consumed.

I can't remember what we ate, as I was too enamored of the flashy colors to pay much attention to what might have been crawling across my plate. We left the "Lodge" with full stomachs, and for me at least, with a sense of loss at the full Anglicization of First Nations People's (Native American) cultures.

A short time after departing, we were "back in the race" in the fullest sense of the term. Our brief hiatus, and even briefer sleep stint, was over. Chaney and Tim took back to the road well, and they both looked strong as they took their turns, one after the other, "leapfrogging" down US 64 West. And that was that. We left Taos almost as soon as we had entered it. There was no time for sightseeing, no time for much of anything. This was, after all, a race.

We cruised down the road, watching Tim and Chaney's rear ends, first one, then the other. We played music for them over the loudspeakers. Chaney's preference was widely varied, from techno to Bob Dylan. Tim's tastes were a bit more transcendent, and he favored Krishna Das, a calming and trance inducing spiritual singer with a worldwide cult following. If Chaney didn't like the musical selection played by a crew member, he began telling us by raising his middle finger. Soon Tim followed Chaney's lead. The system of improvised sign language was crude, to say the least, but it worked nevertheless. I like to imagine that the first sign invented was the one for "eff you". Think about it for a minute.

The constant riding began to take a serious toll on the cyclists' bodies at this point in the race. Chaney's crotch (and let me pause here for a moment to reflect on the fact that never, and I mean never, in my life did I think I would be discussing Chaney's crotch), well, his crotch had seen better days than this one. A product called Chamois Butt'r became the shining and shimmering star of Chaney's day, and if one is to compete in the RAAM, I'd advise bringing along a liberal supply, unless that person desired getting his crotch rubbed raw. The bottle that Chaney held close and dear to his crotch read: "The Ultimate Skin Lubricant & Chamois Cream". I'm not completely sure what "chamois cream" is or how they make it, but it worked for Chaney.

We continued on. By this point it started to seem quite natural. It began to feel as if this was what we had always done, what we would always be doing, forever. The entire race began to feel neither good nor bad, just a grand progression of movement, a forever unfolding of what we were meant to do. We kept on US 64, entering Carson National Forest, climbing hills and following their gentle or steep descents, and the road followed the Red River, which we saw only when we crossed it by bridge. It was a slender thing, weaving its way through Graveyard Canyon below. We went through a litany of places with names like Eagle

Nest, Bobcat Pass, and Touch-Me Not Mountain, finally descending through the canyons on the eastern slopes of the Rocky Mountains onto the epic grasslands of the plains. Where the Rockies meet the Plains may very well be one of the most dramatic scenes I've ever seen. During our last descent, it began raining, and somehow this seemed fitting for our departure from the Rockies, as if nature itself was weeping a goodbye. It was the first time during the trip, and would be the last, that we would see a drop of rain.

Tim rode many of the downhill portions through our steep and dramatic exit from the Rockies, and much of his time was spent going tremendously fast, downhill, through sheets of rain. The roads were slick, rough, and deadly dangerous. One false move and he could be a goner for sure. On one particularly memorable return to the van for his "off time", I asked Tim about how it was on the road in the rain. He'd been out for a good hour of pedaling in fairly steady precipitation. Between gulps from his water bottle, he replied, "Oh, I hadn't realized that it was raining. In fact, right now I have no memory of anything at all." I didn't really know what to say, and feeling that it's often better to say nothing at all, I smiled and nodded as I watched Tim literally tear the lid off the cooler in an effort to find food. He ate whatever his hands landed on, with an avidity that bordered on animal intensity. I was careful to keep my hands away from his mouth.

After this brief episode, we passed through Springer and Clayton, both basically empty towns in New Mexico, and finally arrived in Elkhart, Kansas. According to the folks at RAAM headquarters, Elkhart contains what might very well be the "easiest" portion of the race, a section, "averaging less than 7 feet of climbing per mile". After clipping through the corner of Oklahoma, which seemed to pass faster than taking a breath, we were back in Kansas, where the local time changed from Mountain Daylight to Central Daylight, not that it mattered too much to us by this point. In fact, nothing began to matter very much, at least to me. We had all adjusted to RAAM time, and besides, no one gave a good God damn anymore whether it was night or day, and looking back at it all it's difficult to remember.

It came, I must admit, as somewhat of a shock to me that some of the most beautiful land in the United States is in Kansas. I'm sure that if I had asked, many Kansans would have told me that they knew this long ago, that it was obvious and self-evident, and that any damn fool, even me, could've figured it out with one glance at Kiowa National Grassland and Blanca National Grassland. The National Grasslands were never on my list of places to visit, and never in my life would I have said, "You know, those grasslands are a National Treasure." But let me tell you something, they are. I'm not sure if it is the massive expansiveness of the grasslands or the lack of visual cues that lead to spatial awareness, but something is magical about the grasslands. I don't use that word, "magical", a lot, and I don't use it lightly. Together, the grasslands cover just under 400,000 acres (399, 766, give or take a few). Somewhere in the middle of all that sprawling and waving grass, LaBelle and Lake took over, and our van and the support RV stopped for a much needed mini vacation. And by vacation, I mean brief bursts of micro-sleep, the ingesting of anything edible, and the fixing of mechanical issues with the bikes.

After being newly baptized by the emptiness of the grasslands, I decided to return to the more mundane plane of "where the hell are we going now" consciousness. The descent from the high epiphany to low "where's a sandwich" consciousness came abruptly and harshly. I slumped in the "dining area" of the RV, slathered some organic peanut butter on cheap white bread and washed the whole lot down with, yep, you guessed it, lukewarm wake up juice. Another highlight in life. After this culinary masterpiece, I pulled out the RAAM Route Bible and turned to the portion devoted to Kansas. We were headed directly into "Tornado Alley".

Thirty-Four

In "Tornado Alley", we threaded our way through cornfields, cornrows, endless miles of scorched earth, fields like staccato blasts on horns of emptiness, nothing to keep us going but the Pan-American mantra of "go pedal man go." And at the bottom of it all, a desire like none other to race like all hell to the edge of the earth and drop off into nothingness.

Then, a hotel, a shower, another stop, gas, munchies, donuts, hamburgers, french fries, soda and coffee, people staring, cars honking, near misses and near hits with death on the sidelines shouting, and at the bottom of it arguments and videos recording it all, until nearly underwater I rose and surfaced to see a crack of daylight barely visible through my swollen eyes. We passed Kansas like a hot whirlwind dust storm and clouds upon my eyelids.

Cornrows and combines, dust in the air like fog, and then off and into Missouri. My consciousness amped up slightly in Missouri, just enough to learn what we began to affectionately call the good ol' "Missouri hello!" It's really quite easy to learn, just raise your middle finger and waggle it out your window at each and every cyclist that you see.

Joke: "Whaddya call someone from Missouri?"

Punchline: "An asshole."

Sorry, Missourians, but the image of you as cave dwelling, bushwhacking whack-jobs just ossified a tiny bit more in my mind as I passed through your fart of a state. Without hyperbole, I can say that we got flipped off 10 trillion times going through Missouri. I counted. Honestly, the second best thing about Missouri was hitting a deer with the minivan "Big Business". The minivan made it but the deer, I'm afraid, did not. When we made it to Maryland, there were still tufts of Bambi sticking out from the front bumper, which had been mangled pretty good. The first best thing about Missouri was leaving it. There, I showed you.

959 miles to go. May as well be a million or a billion. By the time we crossed the Mississippi River I was too blinded by deprivations of every kind, sleep, nutrition, spiritual, you name it, to care about how beautiful it was. People often wonder at how explorers can go to the ends of the Earth, to places like Everest, to the poles, to space even, and return with hardly anything to say. I'll tell you, when you're exhausted, tick-bitten, sleep deprived, malnourished, dehydrated, and lacking in every basic social skill or shred of decency you once had, it's damn easy to understand why. I blew by the Mississippi like it was a puddle under our wheels and my vision narrowed to only one thing: get me home, preferably alive.

Illinois, Indiana, Ohio. Where did they go? They went by, road by road, building by building. We leapfrogged down the road, pausing to catch glimpses of landscape, sometimes some food, the occasional stare from a passing motorist. It all became much of the same, a blur of asphalt, a turn of a rubber wheel on the road, a glint in someone's eye, a tear, a fight, another cup of coffee, another person sick, another person tired, another mile, another mile, another mile.

Finally, in West Virginia, something snapped. By the side of the road, somewhere near the aptly named "Warrior Drive" in Cresaptown, Tim Bryant was getting ready to switch off with Chaney, and he mumbled something about needed the crew to take care of his "liquid intake" or something or other like that. Andy Ferrarini, our team medic, snapped. "Tim," he said, "If you say another word about 'liquid intake', I'm going to take that bike and smash it over your fucking head." This was about as heated as it ever got, which isn't so bad, not really anyway. Bryant and Ferrarini are both good guys, really, but the race can bring out both the best and the worst in everyone and anyone. Surprisingly, Bryant said nothing, got on his bike, waited for Chaney to arrive to "cross wheels", and began riding. We were almost there, and I was about to miss the grand finale:

arrival in Annapolis.

It's a sad ending, really it is. I'd be lying if I said I remembered more about those last few states. We did stop to look at some urinals and pick up more burgers at a bar somewhere in West Virginia, or maybe it was somewhere else. The bar advertised "wet t-shirt contests with 'big cash' prizes". I contemplated entering.

I spent the last few states huddled in fetal position.

I was a child of nothingness at the end.

I was sprawled in an impossible position, arms akimbo, waist twisted, legs in opposite directions. I was horizontal more often than I was vertical, useless and helpless. I was tucked away in what we have dubbed the "grandma's attic" of the RV. There were four of us at that point rolling together in the RV down the highway, and we were nearly at the end of our journey. Jim Bernard, crew chief, fearless leader, was driving, hands gripped and blue-knuckled on the steering wheel. I remember flashes of faces. I remember brown eyes and stocky frames, unshaven faces, hands gripping steering wheels, guiding the RV towards the finish line. We had been at this game for just shy of eight days, each of us averaging a mere two hours of sleep in each twenty-four hour period. I can't now say that we were getting two hours a night because we slept where and when we could, during the wee hours of the morning, in the afternoon, on the toilet taking a dump. Sometimes we were on the side of the road, ten thousand feet up in the mountains of Southern Colorado. Other times we were sleeping sitting up in what came to be known as the "best seat" in one of the support vehicles that followed the cyclists, the one on the left hand side of the vehicle, near the sliding door. The right hand seat had been removed for added space, thrown into the jumble of sport equipment behind the rear seats. The "best seat" allowed the extension of legs, and god help me I extended my legs when I could and passed out when I had the chance.

If we were really lucky, we got a resting spot in the RV as it churned down the road at demonical speeds, bouncing on the beds like children who fell on a bounce house floor. Grandma's attic, where I was nestled, was prime real estate. Situs, situs, situs. That's what the real estate folks say it's "all about." The collapsing economy and economic "downturn" became meaningless in dear ol' Grandma's attic, where a soft, five-inch thick mattress and a flattened pillow were the objects I worshiped with a fervor close to madness. The RV lurched and leaped, vomiting the contents of its cabinets onto the floor. And the floor became littered with half-closed trash bags, used batteries, stray backpacks, organic produce falling out of boxes. Before we had left California, Chaney and Tim insisted on shopping at Trader Joe's, picking up roasted almonds, rice, quinoa, various cereals, jams and jellies, peanut butter, cans of sardines, salmon and other smoked fish, soy milk, rice milk, and numerous other high-end, organic produce. Next to those savory items that were now scattered across the floor were pressurized canisters of squirtable "cheese", squirtable grape and strawberry jelly, loaves of processed white bread, wrappers from Big Macs, bottles of Coke, Sprite, and Dr. Pepper.

We were a motley crew and our culinary habits attested to the spectrum of our gustatory desires and financial standings. But Grandma's attic, which became my home at the end, which I had commandeered at the expense of many other crew members, remained relatively stable, pitching and yawing, to be sure, but only a few degrees in any direction at any given time. I slipped in and out of something very loosely resembling sleep in those last states, and I started, at one particularly low point, to imagine that Jim Bernard had become some sort of maniacal automaton, programmed only to proceed from point A to point B without consideration for his own safety or the safety of his passengers. Craig Mace, crew member and police officer on the trip, rode "shotgun".

I began to imagine that he was Jim's accomplice. There was a small, sliding window that was near my head, left open by a former tenant's hand, and though I was, at the moment, freezing, I could not for the life of me figure out how the mechanism worked. This is what it is like at the end. I fumbled with the latch and pushed to the side, feeling the smooth aluminum in my hand.

My fingers ran the length of the latch a few times, the lightness of the metal seeming to yield to a tender touch. Then, resting my hand palm down on the glass, I pressed ever so slightly and my flesh began to tingle. I attempted to push the window again, and it was with considerable difficulty that I realized that the feeling was heat. The glass was warm, smooth, flickering with lights of the passing motorists. The warmth spread from my hand and I swear into my brain, and I had a dim realization that I was headed towards the finish line and it was late June, and I could no longer remember the correct date and no longer cared either way whether I made it or not. It was summer and the weather was beautiful. I was cold but shouldn't be. I was also possessed with a horrific idea at one point that we were hurtling towards a bridge that had a clearance of 9 feet. The RV was at least twelve feet tall. 3 feet too much, my friends, 3 feet too much. I couldn't shake the idea. It had become part of the fabric of my consciousness, a part of my fingers touching the rattling glass, a part of my body cramped into the shrinking space, with the rushing wind that ceaselessly whispered to me. The vehicle would, and of this I was convinced beyond all doubt, careen through the narrow opening under the bridge at nearly seventy (may as well be a trillion) miles per hour. Sparks would fly off both sides into the windy night, cascading to the pavement and illuminating the windy night.

The wind's warm fingers would reach through the windows and caress my hair, shivers rippling through my skin. Bumps formed on my arms, and the acrid taste of bile rose in my throat. Grandma's attic was going to hit the underside of the bridge before anything else. From the exterior, it would look comical, like a cartoon, and the top of the RV will collapse in on itself like a tin can, flimsy, insubstantial. Inside, at the moment of impact, I would have the vague sensation of movement, and the inkling that something had gone wrong. Then, with a terrible swiftness, I would be pushed hard against the side of the upper cabinets on my right-hand side. I would be decapitated, my body thrown limply and swiftly through the dark night air, sending a cascade of my blood over the detritus that has accumulated in the RV during the last days. There I would lie, among the organic produce and crappy white bread. The wind would just keep whispering, and my wife would get the "call" in the middle of the night, say around two A.M. She would realize first that I am gone; then she would curse me for my idiotic behavior, for my lack of foresight (no life insurance, etc). She would lose everything, the house, the cars, and she would be left to raise the children, utterly alone. I have become a real bastard, I thought to myself.

I hallucinated all this, and the images became more or less real, varying in degrees of vividness with my fever. I alternated between being aware of my newfound lunacy and aware that my thoughts were absolute truth. A line occurred to me from an Emily Dickinson poem: "Much madness is divinest sense, to the discerning eye." Perhaps madness is sometimes just madness. The sweat continued to form on my forehead, my back produced a steady crop of dampness, my stomach did strange pirouettes, and my mind finally came totally detached from my body, which had become in turn impossibly numb and alert at the same time.

I felt around my head for my baseball cap, as if somehow it would free me from the imbecility into which I had descended. I felt for it and finally grasped its soft edges, turning it until the bill was in my hands. Then I ran my fingers over the embroidery of the front, where the logo of the race was emblazoned. The image of the logo formed in my mind. *RAAM, The World's Toughest Bicycle Race.* Yep. Bike race from hell. I thought at that moment that I could push the cap over my head to prevent my mind from escaping. It was too late. I was a stone, thrown and careening through darkness, heavy and free.

I found a jumble of sleeping bags along my left side and near my feet. Each one felt like a rock, the downy softness somehow converted by my fever into obsidian hardness, sharp and cutting. I rolled to my right, where the edge dropped off into the RV. It was at most a five foot drop, but I recoiled at it like it was the abyss of Hell. At the bottom, in the incandescent light emanating from above the dining room table, I saw Ed sprawled across the second best bed of the RV. His long frame was stretched from the head of the bed, nearest me, to the foot, where his feet dangled loosely into the air.

His hat was pushed down over his eyes, and his breathing looked steady, relaxed. His large and full mustache rose above a cornfield of grey flecked black stubble. He had become a Buddha in disguise. Above me, centered on the roof was the sole roof vent in the attic, a twelve by twelve plastic bubble sanded to opaque milkiness by the grit of the highway winds. It was open slightly, and the night air whooshed through, carrying strange whispers of my mortality. Soul vent. I tried to shut it, but like the window, it was unwilling to cooperate. I wanted to make it stop its incessant chattering, but it just kept murmuring over and over, *peer into the darkness, peer over the edge, come into the darkness, come closer.*

I had come nearly three-thousand miles, for this, to find the truth. All of us pushed across the empty expanse of the country for truth. We had been through deserts when the moon was nearly gone and the rattlesnakes chattered along the sides of the road in the midnight desert. WE had seen men crushed by the misery of physical defeat and they cycled for hours, and we had seen them lifted by adrenal illumination in the face of challenges that most of us, before this trip, could've scarcely comprehended. But at the end of the trip, as I huddled in hallucinogenic fever, I had become one with the wind rushing through the vent above. I had seen the face of fear and death in the eyes of others and tasted it with my own mouth, and there was nothing but darkness, an eternal expansiveness. Even in the cramped space of the attic I could feel it, whispering, calling me steadily onward. I had become part of the stars and the silence, a member of the family of souls that stretches from California to Maryland, from coast to coast. We went in search of something real and something ethereal, something ineffable and inextinguishable. I had touched the darkness, as all of us on the trip had, and have found that this is what the journey and the destination are about, reaching that unknowable place, where there is no time, no self, no misconception about place, for place has no relevance. It was a state of fear and animal intelligence, of knowing that there is something more, a life force, an energy, a God. Call it what you will, but it was there, hovering all around me, waiting for me to slip into the darkness and the light.

Made in the USA
Lexington, KY
27 June 2014.